AFGHANISTAN
India's Strategic Stakes

AFGHANISTAN

India's Strategic Stakes

Centre for Joint Warfare Studies

HAR-ANAND
PUBLICATIONS PVT LTD

HAR-ANAND PUBLICATIONS PVT LTD
E-49/3, Okhla Industrial Area, Phase-II, New Delhi-110020
Tel.: 41603490 Fax: 011-41708607
E-mail: info@haranandpublications.com
Website: www.haranandpublications.com

First Published: 2010

Published by Ashok Gosain and Ashish Gosain for
Har-Anand Publications Pvt Ltd

Printed in India at Vishal Binding House.

Foreword

The events of 9/11 and the subsequent wars in Iraq and Afghanistan have witnessed political and social turbulence in the region with optimism blooming slowly, but surely, after the US and its allies scrambled for tactical as well as moral support from the regional players. Today a skeptical world community has no illusions about the proclivity of the fundamentalist Jehadis to spell doom for those who are striving to bring about a cultural and social revolution in Afghanistan.

The geostrategic location of Afghanistan and consequent security implications of instability stemming from fears of it being christened as "failed state" force us in India to study the convoluted, tortuous and byzantine contours with caution and prudence. Considering the importance and urgency in addressing the "Af-Pak Issue" the Centre for Joint Warfare Studies embarked upon this venture of sponsoring a study on Afghanistan and India's strategic stakes thereof. The study is based on a scientific Net Assessment of the situation in Afghanistan and India's critical stakes in this region and has been a collective effort of the CENJOWS and the team of eminent contributors headed by Maj Gen (Retd) G D Bakshi, SM, VSM, who himself has been an avid reader and a prolific writer.

There are several issues in this study that stare at the reader. First, the study examines the Barnett Rubin Thesis of Afghanistan as a rentier state and illustrates the destruction of agro-based Afghan economy by Mongols in the 13th Century and the later atrophy of the Silk Route. Second, it focuses on the extraordinary efforts that the Soviets had to resort to in order to protect their lines of communication. The Soviets, who had attempted to win the war with their concept of high tempo, high speed and manoeuvre warfare had to re-arm, re-organize and re-structure to fight the guerilla warfare. The Soviet withdrawal demonstrated that high technology and overwhelming combat power may pummel and batter the opponent but there are numerous other psychological and socio-political fixes that play their role in the final outcome of a conflict. This study provides a comprehensive look at how a modern, high tech force attempted to fight a guerilla war on rugged terrain in the middle of someone else's civil war as opposed to the military books which only deal with the strategy or tactics of a particular war and ignore the vital issues of force structure, branch missions, combat support and combat service support. Third, the study has analysed the current military situation in Afghanistan and highlights how deliberate under-funding and severe under-resourcing of this war has allowed Taliban and Al Qaida to stage a comeback and has been explained with the trend analysis of kinetic events in the recent past.

Besides these, the authors have tried to erase much of awkwardness and haze that prevails about the developments in Afghanistan over the past few decades and the socio-political upheavals and cataclysm that this country has witnessed for almost half a century. While it would be appropriate to acknowledge that the book attempts to provide most of what one wants to know i.e. the history of foreign intervention, the rentier state status, the depredations of warlords and the Taliban, the Russian occupation and exit, the stultifying and stifle internal turmoil over the past couple of decades; it (book) captures neither all relevant perspectives nor all relevant topics. It only attempts at offering nuanced, personal and well considered views of some of the professionals who have rich experience. However, CENJOWS does not in any form endorse, support or propagate their views.

In the end, I, on behalf of the CENJOWS fraternity wish to compliment the study team for their cerebral acumen and intellect at compiling this study report that should stir the minds of the readers and assist them in understanding the implications of the Afghanistan problem, both globally as well as regionally.

K B KAPOOR
Maj Gen (Retd)
Director CENJOWS

Contributors

Maj Gen (Retd) G D Bakshi, SM, VSM is an officer with extensive combat experience in J&K. He served two tenures in the prestigious Military Operations Directorate and taught at the IMA, Defence Services Staff College and the National Defense College at Delhi. He holds a Masters degree and a M. Phil in Defense and Strategic Studies from the University of Madras. Currently he is doing his Ph.D. He has published 18 books and over 80 papers in professional Journals. His book *'Afghanistan: The First Fault Line War'* was widely acclaimed for its research and insight.

Maj Gen (Retd) Abhay Gupta is a highly experienced officer. He holds a Masters and a M Phil degree from the University of Madras and taught at the Defence Services Staff College. As IG Operations of the NSG he provided leadership during the Mumbai Counter terrorist operations. He has travelled widely in Afghanistan and visited Kabul, Jalalabad and Mazar-e-Sharief in 2009.

Brig (Retd) Rahul Bhonsle, SM is a former Infantry Officer with extensive experience in Counter Terrorist Operations. He is a reputed Military Analyst with several Books and Papers to his credit. His latest book is on "Mumbai 26/11: Security Imperatives for the Future." He has done numerous studies on security subjects and is currently a Research Scholar with USI on International Terrorism. He has participated in several national and international Seminars on Security issues.

Col (Retd) Gautam Das is a former officer of the Infantry (11 Gorkha Rifles). During the Sardar Mohammad Regime he had assisted in the training of ANA Officers. He taught Afghan Army and Air Force officers at the Military Intelligence School. He served on deputation to the Ministry of Home Affairs with specialized Counter-Insurgency troops as also with the Cabinet Secretariat with the Special Frontier Force. A prolific writer he has several books and papers to his credit. He has been with the corporate sector for over two decades.

Monika Chansoria, is a Ph.D in International Relations from the Jawahar Lal Nehru University. She pursued post doctoral studies in France (Paris) as the Hermes Post Doctoral Fellow at the Foundation Maison des Sciences de l'Homme and Centre d'etudes et de Recherches Internationales. A prolific writer, her latest Book is titled 'Chinese WMD Proliferation in Asia: US Response'. She earlier participated in a Net Assessment on Iran. She is currently a Research Fellow at the Centre for Land Warfare Studies (CLAWS), New Delhi.

Contents

1

Pattern Recognition: The Rentier State Syndrome of Afghan History

1

Pattern Recognition: The Rentier State Syndrome of Afghan History

BRIEF HISTORICAL SURVEY

Heuristic (as opposed to Algorithmic) forecasts in the domain of National Security can only be made on the basis of the identification of Historical patterns that tend to persist and repeat themselves cyclically. The pattern stands out so clearly in Afghan history. Land-locked Afghanistan has always been the traditional invasion route to the Indian subcontinent. All 'over-land' invasions of the subcontinent have come via the key Afghan passes of Khyber and Bolan. This saga of invasions goes back to the millennium before the Birth of Christ and includes Alexander the Great's invasion (326 BC) and subsequent invasions by the Huns, Sakas, Scythians, Mongols, Mughals and Safavids. After unification by Ahmad Shah Abdali, the Afghan tribes themselves launched major military expeditions for loot and occupied large tracts of northern India. The region now included in Afghanistan was a border land between empires that ruled from India, Iran or Central Asia. It is an arid shatter zone of endemic conflict.

The Rentier State Barnett Rubin, the foremost American expert on Afghanistan, has put forward the thesis of Afghanistan as 'rentier state'. It is a state with no indigenous natural/agricultural base that could sustain state formation. Inevitably, national consolidation in Afghanistan has occurred with massive economic and military aid from external powers. The rentier state so installed has exercised minimal control over the tribes by distributing the economic largesse. The state has never been able to penetrate fully the fragmented tribal society and draw up a sustainable structure for tax collection/local government.

The region that comprises Afghanistan was the borderland between empires that ruled from India, Iran and Central Asia. Its history, therefore, represents the ebb and flow of these empires. In 305 BC Chandragupta Maurya inflicted a crushing defeat on the Greek armies of Seleucus and captured Afghanistan. Thus, the Mauryans were the first empire-builders to recognize the strategic importance of Afghanistan. Vincent Smith writes "The first Indian emperor, more than two thousand years ago, thus entered into possession of that scientific frontier, sighed for in vain by his English successors and never held in its entirety by the Mughal monarchs of the sixteenth and seventeenth centuries."

In the Mauryan period, Afghanistan was an outpost of the Indian empire and a prime centre for Buddhist art and thought. The Gandhara School which resulted from a fusion of Indo-Greek styles was based in Afghanistan. Buddhism flourished in Afghanistan both under Ashoka and the Kushans. The 53 meter tall Buddha idol at Bamiyan, northwest of Kabul (that was so thoughtlessly destroyed by the Taliban), bore ample testimony to the Buddhist influence. Afghanistan even finds mention in the ancient epic 'Mahabharata', once again as Gandhara; its ruling families being depicted as playing an active role in the sub-continental politics even in that ancient period. Olaf Caroe states in his book, "The Pathans 550 BC to 1957" that the Hindu Shahi dynasty ruled in Afghanistan from AD 400 to 900. It was thereafter conquered by the Arabs and Islam spread to Afghanistan.

Rentier Economy: Afghanistan, however, has always been a wasteland and ideal buffer between empires. Only 12 percent of its land area is arable, but on account of scarcity of water, only half of this area is cultivated in a year. The local people had constructed a system of open and underground canals (called 'Karez' in Pashto). The crop thus produced barely sustained the local population, through a barter system between nomads and the peasants. The nomads, inhabitants of the hill pastures, are called Nang Pashtun; and the peasants who live in the valleys are called the Qualang Pashtuns. The nomadic tribes have hardly ever been brought under the control of any regime in Afghanistan.

Most nation-states draw their national income from taxation of the local population. Thus at the time of the French Revolution in 1789, 85 per cent of France's population were peasants. Agriculture accounted for 60 per cent of production. The French peasants bore the brunt of the tax burden. In 1978, Afghanistan also had 85 per cent population as peasants or nomads and agriculture accounted for 60 per cent of the national produce. But the Afghan peasants paid virtually no taxes.

The Silk Route Trade: Historically the Afghan economy was sustained largely by its primitive agriculture and pastoral activities and by taxes levied on the Silk Route trade that passed through Afghanistan.

The Destruction of the Afghan Economy: The conquest of this region by the Mongol armies of the dreaded Genghiz Khan in the thirteenth century proved to be a historical disaster for Afghanistan. The Mongols destroyed the Afghan irrigation system and the flourishing cities of Central Asia which were the centres of trade and commerce between Asia, Europe and the Middle East. The Mongol conquests and depredation seriously dislocated the trade and commerce activities in inner Asia. Subsequently the opening of the sea route between Europe and Asia in the fifteenth century sent this region into a steep historical decline. The Silk Route atrophied. Deprived of its toll revenues, Afghanistan could no longer be an economically viable state. Most of its population reverted to nomadism thereafter.

Sixteenth Century—Gun Powder Empires: The decline of the Mongols was followed by the rise of the Turko-Mongol "gun- powder empires." These militarized tribes exploited the Chinese invention of gunpowder and the Mongol invention of the stirrup to bring forth very efficient and mobile cavalry armies. The Ottomans, the Safavids, the Shayabanid Uzbeks and the Mughals fought for the domination and control of the Western and Inner Asian landmass. The Mughals ultimately conquered Afghanistan and later succeeded in establishing a mighty empire in the subcontinent that included Afghanistan as an outlying province.

Eighteenth Century—Rise of Pashtuns: The Turko-Mongol tribes (the Safavids and the Mughals) imposed their militarized tribal organizational models on the Pashtun tribes of Afghanistan. The Pashtun tribal lashkars (cavalry) was strengthened by years of service to the Mughals and later the Safavids. Once the Turko-Mongol tribes declined in the eighteenth century, however, a group of Pashtun tribes (the Abdalis, the Ghilzai and their sub-tribes the Durranis, Saddozais, Muhammadzais and Hotakis) founded their own empire. This Afghan state drew its economic resources from conquest and loot of the surrounding richer areas, especially in India. Like other tribal conquest empires, this proved unstable. Once the charismatic leader (Ahmad Shah Abdali) passed from the scene and loot declined, this tribal state split up into feuding tribes once again.

Ahmad Khan (later Ahmad Shah Abdali) effected the first state consolidation in Afghanistan in recent history. The Safavid rulers of Iran had structured the Abdali and Ghilzai tribes into large-scale military organizations. The Abdalis were part of the Turkic Nadir Shah Afshar's armies that ranged as far as Delhi and brought about the destruction of the Mughal Empire in India. After Nadir Shah's assassination, Ahmad Shah was chosen as the leader of the Abdali tribe. To his tremendous good fortune he was able to loot a caravan transporting Nadir Shah's taxes back to Iran. This economic windfall financed the initial alliances and military efforts of Ahmad Shah. Thus, even the first Afghan state in recent history was raised with external economic resources.

Ahmad Shah later unified all the Pashtun tribes. The combination of a highly charismatic military leader and the sharing of loot cemented group feelings and overcame tribal rivalry. Over three-fourths of this state's income came from conquests and loot in India, mainly in the Punjab and Kashmir provinces. Because he extracted wealth from external sources, Ahmad Shah did not face the problem of how to extract resources from the tribes on whom he depended for military power.

Ahmad Shah's kingdom disintegrated after his death. The Sikh empire of Ranjit Singh consolidated its hold in the Punjab and captured Peshawar. Some of Ranjit Singh's Generals like Hari Singh Nalwa and Gulab Singh reached as far as Jalalabad. The loss of the Indian territories deprived the Saddozai Pashtun rulers of the wealth which had enabled them to cement their tribal coalition. Tribal warfare split the Afghan Kingdom into several smaller states.

This established the heuristic historical pattern which has since replicated itself several times in Afghanistan. The loss of revenue from outside the territory of Afghanistan has led to a loss of state control and the emergence of regional power centres. This pattern persisted till 1992 when Najibullah fell as a result of the loss of Soviet economic and military support which led to ethnic fragmentation between the Pashtun and Farsiwan tribes and the virtual disintegration of Afghanistan.

Formation of the Modern Afghan State: In 1919 Afghanistan entered the Europe-centered system of modern nation-states of the nineteenth century. This was an outgrowth of the rise of British imperial power in the Indian sub-continent and the Russian conquest of Central Asia. Afghanistan now became a neutral state between the British and Russian empires. Thus began the era of the Great Game.

The Anglo-Afghan Wars

The First Anglo-Afghan War (1839-42): This was launched by the British for the outright conquest of Afghanistan. Logistics and under-resourcing proved to be the undoing of this ill fated campaign. This military disaster of the British enabled Dost Mohammad, the Afghan ruler to resume his rule. Dost Mohammad received external aid both from British India and Iran. The British provided weapons in appreciation of his neutrality in the Indian uprising of 1857-59. Dost Mohammad consolidated his hold by playing one tribe off against another and established a nation-state with external economic and military aid.

Russian Thrust in Central Asia: In the reign of Czar Alexander the Second (1855-1881) Russia had begun her imperial power projection into the Caucasus and Central Asia. His Foreign Minister Prince A Gorchakov had given a decisive Eastward orientation to Russian Foreign policy. At its roots was a hunger for a key resource of that era-Cotton! The American Civil War (1861-65) had suddenly cut off supplies of cotton to Russian merchants. They now clamoured to capture the cotton fields of Central Asia. The British were alarmed by the perceived Russian thrust towards the warm water ports of Iran and the Makran coast. They therefore embarked upon a forward policy to check the Russian advance well ahead of their Indian colonial possessions. This was the peak period of British geopolitical concern in Afghanistan.

The Second Anglo-Afghan War (1878-80): Resulted from this era of peak British security concern about Afghanistan, fuelled by the Russian thrust into Central Asia. The British launched a second military invasion which resulted in a partial victory for the Afghans, who maintained their internal sovereignty but ceded their foreign relations to the British. Amir Abdul Rehman Khan (the Iron Amir) seized the Afghan throne after the departure of the British troops.

Thus Afghanistan formally entered the state system under British suzerainty as a buffer state against Russia which emerged after the two Anglo-Afghan wars. The British lavished weapons and cash on Amir Abdul Rehman Khan (1881-1901). Rehman Khan used these coercive resources to establish the basic state structure that endured till the fall of Najibullah in 1992. *The essential contours of this state structure have basically involved a Pashtun ruler using external resources to reign over an ethnically heterogeneous society while manipulating the social segmentation to weaken the tribal societies' resistance to his rule. (Rubin)*

Third Anglo-Afghan War in 1919: The significantly high level of British security concern in Afghanistan is highlighted by their launching the Third Anglo-Afghan War in 1919. Rehman's grandson Amanullah Khan had tried to exploit the weakened condition of the British and Russians after World War I. He announced independence for his country which led to the brief war. However unlike Turkey's Kemal Attaturk or Reza Shah of Iran, Amanullah Khan could not transform his country into a modern autocracy. Afghanistan lacked any national organizations/parties or institutions (like the Indian National Congress) and had no articulate/educated middle class.

Amanullah, the modernizer, was overthrown by a tribal rebellion. Subsequently anarchy broke out in Afghanistan. Nadir Khan (one of Amanullah's Generals) then established Pashtun rule in Kabul. Nadir Khan was appointed Shah in Kabul and the reign of the Musahiban dynasty commenced in 1929, which lasted till 1978.

Nadir Khan was succeeded in 1933 by Zahir Shah. Right through World War II the British kept on anticipating an Axis threat to their Indian possessions via Afghanistan. The Japanese invasion, however, came via Burma and belied all geopolitical formulations of the heartland theorists. The British Indian Army had been facing the wrong strategic direction and training for a war that never came. This was primarily because the Soviet Union and Britain became allies in World War II. The very rationale of the Great Game was thus negated.

Post-Colonial Afghanistan

The end of the British Empire saw the partition of the subcontinent into India and Pakistan. Pakistan and Russia (USSR) became the two main neighbours of Afghanistan. The USSR then was a superpower and regarded Afghanistan as very much in her legitimate sphere of influence.

In 1973, Zahir Shah was deposed by his uncle Mohammed Daoud Khan who appointed himself President, with Zahir Shah taking exile in Rome. The British external support was now largely replaced by Soviet economic and military aid. Thus between 1955 and 1978, the USSR provided Afghanistan $1.25 billion in economic and approximately $1.27 billion in military aid. The rentier state pattern continued albeit with changed external patrons. The key fact that merits highlighting however is that between 1919 when the third Afghan War was fought and 1979, the year of the Soviet invasion, for nearly six decades Afghanistan had functioned as a viable and fairly self sufficient state that could feed its sparse population and towards the end was sustaining a fairly modern armed force of an impressive strength of some 350,000. Afghanistan exports of dry fruits then amounted to some 65% of the world's trade in this commodity and its Natural Gas exports were earning some $ 300 million per year. The Soviet invasion of Afghanistan in 1979 brought about a significant paradigm shift in this region. It destroyed the traditional neutrality of Afghanistan. *Afghanistan was rapidly transformed from a buffer state to a tragically failed state.* Elizabeth Gould and Paul Fitzgerald write that the US used Afghanistan as a sacrificial arena to give the Soviets their Vietnam. This was done in the form of the most ambitious and expensive covert operations in recent history where billions of dollars were funneled in via Pakistan's ISI to train and induct some 80,000 Afghan Mujahideen and some 30,000 Arab and North African Jihadis. This Jihad ideology destroyed one of the oldest nation states in Asia. This has caused the most unfathomable humanitarian catastrophes in modern history as would be evident from the following details:

- One million Afghans have been killed in these wars and some four million wounded and maimed for life.
- Five million Afghans have become refugees in Iran and Pakistan.
- Two million Afghans have become internally displaced due to the fighting.
- The enormity of these statistics can fully be grasped only when we juxtapose these casualties against the overall population of Afghanistan in 1979- just 15 million.
- Small wonder that recent visitors to Afghanistan have reported a strong yearning to regain their lost nationhood amongst the Afghan people.

PATTERN RECOGNITION

The heuristic patterns that emerge from this brief historical survey of state formation and collapse are summarized below:-

Rentier State: Only 12 per cent of the land area of Afghanistan is arable. This problem is further compounded by scarcity of water. Thus Afghanistan has traditionally lacked a viable economic basis for nationhood. Economic resources for nation-building have traditionally been provided by external sources, which included:

- Taxation of caravans plying the Silk Route.
- Loot from tribal conquest of richer surrounding areas in India and Iran.
- Large-scale external military and economic aid to prop up a chosen regime in Afghanistan. In the Great Game period this was provided by the British as aid. In the post-war period the Soviet Union stepped in to impose and prop up regimes of its choice. Currently this is being done by the USA.

Tribe versus State: The tribe predates the state as an anthropological and political phenomenon. The state (including the foreign backed rentier state) was never able to penetrate the Afghan society in any comprehensive manner. Though 85 per cent of the Afghan population comprised peasants and nomads and 60 percent of the state's product was from agriculture the peasants and nomads hardly ever paid taxes. At best the Afghan state was able to tax the Qualang Afghan peasants of the river valleys. The Nang Pashtuns nomads of the hill regions were always beyond the pale of the Afghan state.

The Patterns of Change: Keeping these distinct factors as the backdrop, the historical pattern of state formation and collapse in Afghanistan has conformed to the following model:

- A charismatic military leader uniting the tribes with promise of loot, with his rule being based on coercive power acquired as a result of foreign military and economic aid/resources
- Generally this has involved a Pashtun ruler using external resources to reign over an ethnically heterogeneous society, while manipulating that social segmentation to weaken the tribal societies' resistance to his rule.
- The demise of the charismatic leader and or more usually the end of foreign economic aid/external resources has led to a break-up of the Afghan state along ethnic and tribal faultlines.
- This pattern is visible throughout the period from 1747 (when Ahmad Shah Abdali, the charismatic Shah Baba) established the first unified Afghan state in recent history, to the latest example of Soviet-backed state formation and disintegration in Afghanistan that occurred in 1992 with the fall of Najibullah.
- The Barnett Rubin thesis of a rentier state in Afghanistan however needs to be qualified by the caveat that post 1919, there was a functional and viable nation state in Afghanistan that served as a buffer state between the British and Russian Empires. This buffer state was destroyed by the violent clash of super power interests that began with the Soviet invasion of Afghanistan. The Americans and Saudis funded the most expensive covert war campaign in history to cause attrition to Soviet forces in Afghanistan. In the bargain, one of the oldest nation states of Asia was comprehensively destroyed by using the anti-state ideology of Jihad. Via the Taliban, Pakistan has tried to ensure that Afghanistan does not become a normal nation state again but remains a Somalia analogue in South West Asia.
- This brief survey of Afghan history should therefore serve to throw sufficient light on the pattern of rentier state formation and collapse

in Afghanistan. This pattern serves as a useful tool for making heuristic forecasts/prognostications about thc futurc course of events in Afghanistan. The rationale is simple. Historical patterns have a tendency to persist and repeat themselves in a cyclical pattern. Hence a study of the patterns of the past serves to provide a fairly reliable basis for making Heuristic forecasts about the nature of future changes.

It is obvious that the resuscitation of the nation state in Afghanistan will entail sustained engagement by the international community and the provision of extensive economic and financial assistance. Unfortunately donor fatigue is already visible. The US alone has provided some US$32 billion in assistance (to include approximately $15 billion for raising the Afghan National Army and Police). All other countries(to include Japan, EU, Canada, China, India etc) have given some $50 billion. India has provided economic and infrastructural assistance worth over a billion US Dollars. US Defense Secretary Robert Gates disclosed recently that the annual revenue of the Afghan State is just $700 million. Sustaining the costs of a 134,000 strong Afghan army itself would cost $2billion a year. This gives an indication of the extent of financial support the Afghan state will need in the foreseeable future. The only answer is to make it financially viable by encouraging high-value agriculture in its limited arable areas (by way of expensive dry fruits, Pomegranates etc). The Afghan economy must develop strong linkages with the more vibrant Indian economy where it will find ready markets for its high-value agricultural products and mineral wealth. The Silk Route to Central Asia and India must be revived by routing oil and natural gas pipelines from Central Asia to Iran and Pakistan via Afghanistan. Pakistan unfortunately has been doing its best to prevent establishment of structural linkages between the Indian and Afghan economies. This is a ploy to prevent the stabilisation of a viable state in Afghanistan.

REFERENCES

1. Barnett R Rubin *The Fragmentation of Afghanistan; State Formation and Collapse in the International System.* Yale University Press. 1995. p. 81.
2. *Ibid,* p. 46.

3. *Ibid,* p. 50.
4. *Ibid,* p. 19.
5. Admic Ludwig *1900-1923:A Diplomatic History.* University of California Press. Berkely.
6. Daniel Markey, *From Af-Pak to Pak-Af: A Response to the New US Af-Pak Strategy for South Asia. Council of Foreign Relations.* Policy Option Papers. New York. April 2009.
7. Olaf Caroe, *The Pathans: 500BC-1957AD,* Keegan Paul International. London 1958. (2000 Reprint).
8. Jill Crystal, *Oil and Politics in the Gulf; Rulers and Merchants in Kuwait and Qatar.* Cambridge University Press. 1990. (For a comprehensive treatment of the concept of a Rentier state).

2

Soviet Invasion and Afghan Resistance: Military Models and Evaluation Templates for the Ongoing Counter Insurgency Campaign

The change of circumstances in the international system gave the Afghan state far greater autonomy. Britain withdrew from India, leaving the new nation of Pakistan on one border of Afghanistan while the Soviet Union across another border emerged as a superpower after World War II. It became one of the poles of a bipolar world. Soviet influence over Afghanistan was bound to increase with the absence of the countervailing British imperial power.

THE AFGHAN-PAK DISPUTE: THE PASHTUN QUESTION

When British India became independent as India and Pakistan, the Afghans argued that the tribal areas should have been given the option of declaring independence (as Pashtunistan) or joining Afghanistan. Instead the colonial authority gave them the choice of opting for either India or Pakistan: they chose the latter. Thus from the very inception of Pakistan, the new state was set on a collision course with its neighbor to the north-west. Afghanistan, in fact, opposed Pakistan's membership of the UNO. Being a land-locked country, Afghanistan was dependant on Pakistan for outlet to the sea via the port of Karachi. The resentment and fear that the Pashtunistan issue raised in the Punjab military rulers of Pakistan caused a sharp deterioration in relations as Pakistan tried to restrict Afghanistan's access to the sea.

In 1950 the Pakistani rulers started a slowdown of trade/commercial traffic from the seaport to Afghanistan, In retaliation for Afghanistan raising the Pashtun issue. Afghanistan tried to seek alternative routes to the sea via Eastern Iran. At this juncture, the Soviets came to the assistance of Afghanistan and Soviet-Afghan relations warmed up.

Afghanistan had initially sought assistance from USA. This was available only in small amounts and after Pakistan joined the CENTO and SEATO alliances and received large-scale military aid from the USA, this source dried up. John Foster Dulles refused military aid to Afghanistan in 1954. A month later the Afghan government accepted the Soviet offer of military and economic assistance.

The international realignment now saw India and Afghanistan as recipients of military equipment from the Soviet Union while Pakistan became a US military ally. From the geostrategic point of view there has always been a strong convergence of interests between New Delhi and Kabul from the 1950s. The ethnic issue is bound to cause friction between any regime in Afghanistan and Pakistan. To that extent India is a natural ally of Afghanistan vis-à-vis its immediate neighbor Pakistan.

Soviet military and economic assistance grew in volume. From 1954 till 1973, foreign assistance and sale of natural gas to the Soviet Union accounted for 80 per cent of Afghan investment in development expenditure. Afghanistan thus became a weak rentier state now of the USSR. Foreign aid led to a rise in the level of education and literacy. It produced a small but vocal and influential intellectual class of teachers, bureaucrats and military officers.

In 1973 Mohammed Daoud Khan staged a coup, deposing his cousin King Zahir Shah and appointing himself as President. Daoud captured power not as the head of a tribal army but with the help of Soviet-trained military officers. Many of them were members of the Parcham and Khalq factions of the PDPA (People's Democratic Party of Afghanistan). This coup signaled the entry of the intellectuals in the struggle for power between the monarchal state and the tribes.

In 1973, the Persian Gulf and Middle Eastern states received large revenues from the increase in oil prices. Iran, with US help and petrodollars, became a regional power centre. By October 1974 Iran was making overtures to Afghanistan. The Shah of Iran offered aid worth \$2 billion to Kabul, the bulk of it (\$1.7 billion) for a proposed rail road linking Kabul and Ghazni and Kandahar and Herat to the Iranian port of

Bandar Abbas to provide Afghanistan a secure and economical access to the sea via Iran, thereby reducing the Soviet leverage as the only alternative route for Afghan overland trade. This increased Soviet apprehensions.

THE SAUR REVOLUTION

On 27 April 1978, leftist military officers overthrew Mohammed Daoud Khan in a surprise coup and Noor Mohammed Taraki came to power at the head of a PDPA government. Though the pro-Khalq and Parcham military officers were united in staging the coup, the Khalq-Parcham factional feud now came to the fore.

In July 1979, President Taraki virtually exiled the main Parcham leaders by sending them out as ambassadors to various countries. Hafizullah Amin became the new Khalq strongman. For the first time in Afghan history, Amin tried to enforce total government control over the tribes, but he did it in a brutal and ham handed fashion. He tried to enforce land reform and force march a tribal society into socialism. The nascent Afghan state's organizational structure, the army and bureaucracy, were not able or willing to enforce such radical changes in so short a time. The central organs of the fragile Afghan state began to crumble and widespread revolt and rebellion spread amongst the tribes.

The Soviets were alarmed at this reckless pace of reform and the destruction of the organs of the secular Afghan state. They tried to replace Hafizullah Amin with a Taraki-Babrak Karmal coalition. Hafizullah Amin in turn overthrew and killed Taraki and made overtures to the USA. These caused panic in Moscow. Barnett R. Rubin writes that it was at this stage that Leonid Brezhnev, the Soviet strongman, and his key advisers decided to intervene militarily.

The original intention seems to have been *a six-month operation to stabilize the situation and hand it over to the Parchamites. Instead the Soviets got sucked into a quagmire.* Hafizullah Amin's antics had so thoroughly inflamed the Afghan society that the revolt was complete and widespread. By early 1979 armed resistance flared up in twenty five of the twenty eight provinces of Afghanistan. The Afghan army and civil bureaucracy had virtually disintegrated and the Soviet forces were sucked into a war they do not seem to have bargained for originally.

INVASION

The Soviet invasion of Afghanistan was a military masterpiece of careful planning and flawless execution. Excellent accounts of it are available in David C. Isby's *War in a Distant Country: Afghanistan Invasion and Resistance and Anthony Cordesman's Lessons of Modern War, Volume III (Afghanistan).*

The operation of the Termez based Soviet 40th Army was an outstanding military success. The Soviets quickly fanned out to secure the major towns and communication routes. Their concept of operations appeared to be:

- Stabilize the country by garrisoning the main routes, major cities, air bases and logistic sites.
- Relieve the Afghan government garrison forces and push them into the countryside to battle the resistance.
- Provide logistics, air, artillery and intelligence support to the Afghan government forces.
- Strengthen Afghan forces to defeat the resistance, so as to enable Soviet forces to withdraw at the earliest.

AFGHANISTAN COMPARED WITH THE VIETNAM IMBROGLIO

The Afghan General Mohd Yahaya Navroj comments, "The Soviet war in Afghanistan differed significantly from the oft-compared Vietnam War. In Vietnam the US deployment had reached peak strength over 550,000 troops. By comparison, in Afghanistan, a region five times the size of Vietnam, the Soviet strength varied from 90,000 to 120,000 troops. The Soviets four divisions, five independent brigades and three independent regiments of the 40th Army strained their utmost to provide security for the 29 provincial centres and industrial and economic installations and were hard pressed to extend security to thousands of villages, hundreds of miles of road communication routes and key terrain features across the country."

This limitation in Soviet force deployment is difficult to understand and gives an insight into the Soviet economic, infrastructural and societal weakness in that period. The entire thrust of the Soviet strategy was to *hold the key towns and communication infrastructure and rebuild the Afghan Army to take on the insurgents.*

AFGHAN RESISTANCE

The Soviets had been sucked into a quagmire much against their calculations. Hafizullah Amin's brutal methods had totally alienated the Afghan population. The attack on the Islamic religion had infuriated the tribal people. The Afghan Army had strength of three Corps Headquarters, three Independent Armoured Brigades, twelve Infantry Divisions and three Commando Brigades. But massive desertions and mutinies reduced their strength to just 30,000 in 1980. The Afghan government forces had to be virtually rebuilt and retrained from scratch. This took five to six years and the Soviets were stuck.

In Phase-one, the local tribes launched spontaneous rebellions. Soviet military operations caused heavy losses in the countryside and quite systematically destroyed the support infrastructure for Mujahideen operations.

In Phase Two, the Mujahideen tribes and groups began to receive large scale American, Chinese, Saudi and Western military aid through Pakistan. This enabled them to stand up to Soviet military operations. Pakistan officially recognized six parties based in Peshawar as representative of the refugees and the Mujahideen. Iran backed the Shia tribal groups of the Hazaras, Heratis and Nuristanis. Barnett R Rubin writes that *most of the resistance units (56 per cent according to CIA studies) comprised around 20 to 60 men, about the maximum size of units based on face-to face interaction.* The insurgents tended to avoid risky action that might endanger essential economic activities and till the very end, they found it difficult to coordinate large-scale offensives because of disputes over the distribution of booty amongst rival groups.

The ISI became the prime channel for distributing the arms and finances to the Afghan Mujahideen. It tried to promote its own favourites like Hekmatyar and Sayyaff at the cost of the more successful Mujahideen commanders operating inside Afghanistan. Between 1983 and 1987 the ISI provided military training to 80,000 Afghan

Mujahideen. The ISI, writes Rubin, insisted on controlling and directing the military operations of the Mujahideen. It did not permit the emergence of a unified military force but relied on a system of brokerage based on distribution of weapons to parties and small groups of fighters. This strategy exacerbated the social fragmentation of Afghanistan and favoured that category of Mujahideen commanders who conformed to Pakistan's military and political goals. This seriously hampered the Mujahideen war effort and subsequently led to sharp differences between the CIA and the ISI.

Arms and financial aid, however, poured into Afghanistan. By end 1992 Afghanistan had more small arms than the combined armies of India and Pakistan put together. US aid grew from $30 million in 1980. Saudi Arabia matched and slightly exceeded the American contribution. The Chinese contributed by selling Soviet-style weapons to the CIA for transfer to the ISI and the Mujahideen. A massive supply effort was set up by the CIA by sea to Karachi and by air to Islamabad. Only Soviet-style weapons were given initially. It was only in 1986 that American Stingers were provided to overcome the highly effective Hind helicopter gunships of the Soviets.

SOVIET COUNTER GUERILLA OPERATIONS IN AFGHANISTAN

A detailed account of the Soviet operations in Afghanistan from 1980-1989 is essential because it provides useful templates and models on which to evaluate/judge the ongoing US/NATO Counter Insurgency (COIN) operations in that country. For the military professional, the Soviet counter guerilla operations in Afghanistan contain a wealth of information. The overall Soviet force commitment in Afghanistan was curiously restricted in scope and scale. The strategy seemed premised upon holding the cities and communication arteries and employing the Afghan Army for controlling the countryside. The operation was initially designed to last six months. It was aimed at restoring the situation and then handing the control over to the Afghan Army.

Once in, the Soviets realized the Hafizullah Amin's atrocities had alienated the people and destroyed the state institutions of control and governance. It took the Soviets almost one decade to rebuild the Afghan Army, Intelligence agencies and the bureaucracy. In the meantime the limited Soviet contingent of some 120,000 troops strained every nerve to hold a rugged country five times the size of Vietnam. The *hallmark of the Soviet operational style was a heavy reliance on mechanized operations, mounted sweeps and over-reliance on firepower and air power.* The aim was to cut casualties and speed up operations. It was a full-fledged conventional war on the Warsaw pattern with little semblance of low-intensity conflict restraints. In the succeeding paras a chronological record of the Soviet operations is given in some detail so that lessons relevant to the present context can be drawn.

1980

By 1980 the Afghan Army strength had been depleted to just 20,000 due to mass desertions and mutinies. The 8th Afghan Division fought a brief but bitter action with the Soviet forces. The Soviets (after securing the cities and road network) had been pushing out the Afghan Army units for sweeps in the river valleys. The unreliability of the Afghan Army in such operations forced the Soviets to change track. The Soviets were now forced to employ their own Motor Rifle (MR) Divisions for this task. Even the Soviet MR divisions were staffed by poorly trained Muslim reservist troops from Central Asia. They had been chosen as it was felt that they would be more acceptable to the Afghan people. On 21 February 1980, there was a mass uprising in Kabul. The Afghan Army refused to fire on the people and Soviet forces had to move in. Apparently excessive firepower was used. This led to further mutinies in the Afghan Army.

In March-May, September and November 1980 the Soviets launched a massive mechanized sweep into the Kunar valley. The Soviet troops were reluctant to leave their BMPs. They relied upon heavy prophylactic fire and were chary of leaving their vehicles to chase the Mujahideen on foot. They systematically began to destroy the infrastructure in Mujahideen villages, launched major sweeps in Bamiyan province against rebel forces led by Sayed Jaglan (an Afghan Army deserter), and launched massive operations against Ahmed Shah Masood operating in the Panjshir valley. This was done in mounted operations without securing the heights overlooking the road. By end December 1980 the Soviets were forced to induct more Motor Rifle Divisions.

1981

The year 1981 saw a marked shift in the Soviet tactical style. The Soviets abandoned massive sweeps by mechanized columns and instead began to rely upon smaller operations. Increased resort was made to air power. At the tactical level, however, mechanized columns continued to move without securing the heights. There was little patrolling or reconnaissance. The Soviets still relied upon firepower. As a result of experience gained in 1980 the Soviets became more methodical. Mechanized columns now leap-frogged from one fire base to another. These fire bases were 15-20 kilometers apart (which is the range of the BM-21 multi-barrel rocket launcher). Prior to advance, heavy air bombardments and attack helicopter sorties were launched and the mechanized columns moved rapidly between bases.

1982

The Afghan Army was still of limited utility during this period especially in offensive combat. The Soviets had begun a Herculean programme of fresh recruitment and re-training.

In January 1982, the Soviets launched a major offensive in Parwan that annihilated much of the resistance. Similar offensives were launched in Kandahar and Herat. To ensure security of the Kabul-Gardez highway the Soviets began to depopulate the areas around the road. The prime military focus of the Soviet Afghan War was on securing their lines of communication. Thus the heaviest fighting took place against the Tajik guerillas of Ahmad Shah Masood who operated in the Panjshir valley and posed a threat to the strategic Salang tunnel and the Soviet main supply line to Kabul. The geography posed this tactical and operational imperative. The main trade/transit route from Central Asia to Kabul-Jalalabad and Peshawar (Pakistan) runs along the valley draw of the Kabul river (Darya-e-Kabul). The Anderab, Panjshir, Alimgar and Kunar river valleys run at right angles to the main Kabul river and are its tributaries. Hence guerrillas located in these valleys posed a serious threat to the main Kabul road axis.

It was due to this operational imperative that the heaviest fighting of the Afghan War took place in the Panjshir and the parallel valleys. The Soviets launched a series of major operations in this area. In April-May 1982 the Soviets launched Operation Panjshir V. This was the second biggest battle of the war. The Soviets used massive air power and artillery and claimed to have inflicted 10 per cent losses on Ahmad Shah Masood. Masood however retreated to the surrounding ridges and escaped destruction. In September 1982, the Soviets launched Operation Panjshir VI. Masood came under heavy pressure but managed to survive again. Major sweeps were also launched against Phagman, Wardak and Loghar provinces, and the Ghorband valley. The refurbished Afghan Army launched an attack on the Paktia base of the Peshawar based Mujahideen. In December Masood's guerillas blew up the Salang tunnel and caused many casualties.

1983

In late 1982 the Soviets reviewed their battle experience and began to develop an air war doctrine which placed heavy reliance on bombing of villages of the Mujahideen combined with attacks by Hind helicopter gunships (the Mi-24 and Mi-25, which became the nemesis of the guerillas). These were combined with mechanized ground sweeps. As a result of this concerted pressure the KGB negotiated a local truce with Ahmed Shah Masood in March 1983.

The Soviets carried out an intense air bombardment of Kandahar and followed up with a major combined Soviet-Afghan Army offensive to test the re-created Afghan Army and give it more experience. The entire Soviet thrust was to conserve casualties and restrict manpower deployments. Lack of manpower was sought to be compensated by massive application of firepower and increasing use of the re-created Afghan Army.

Herat was re-captured from rebel government forces in 1983. An effective combined arms offensive was launched in the Loger valley. The

Ghazni offensive in June 1983, however, had limited success. In end 1983 the Mujahideen managed to destroy an Afghan Army commando base at Khost. Later Mujahideen groups laid siege to the town of Urgun.

1984

In 1984 the Soviets increased their emphasis on the use of air power. From January 1984 increasing reliance was placed on heli-borne forces. Special Forces units of the Spetsnaz were now dropped at the dominating heights overlooking the valley floors on which major mechanized operations were being launched. Ahmed Shah Masood sensed the preparations that were on and made a pre-emptive strike in March 1984. He ambushed a fuel convoy on the Salang Tunnel and destroyed it. This led to severe fuel shortage in Kabul. The Soviets retaliated with Operation Panjshir VII in April 1984. This was the biggest battle of the entire Afghan War and merits a detailed look for it gives an insight into the Soviet operational techniques. Also, in view of the current ethnic struggle between the Pashtuns and Tajiks, the operation held important military lessons for the Afghan civil war that came after the Soviet withdrawal.

Over 20,000 Soviet troops (mostly paratroopers) took part in the Panjshir VII offensive. Subsequently 6,000 Soviet reinforcements (to include one regiment of the crack 104 Guards Airborne Division) were flown in from Kirovabad. The tally of Soviet units engaged included:

- One regiment ex-104 Guards Airborne Division (Kirovabad)
- 375 regiment ex-105 Guards Airborne Division (now disbanded)
- Two regiments ex-103 Guards Airborne Division (ex- Kabul)
- One regiment ex-108 Motorized Rifle Division (ex-Kabul).

This makes it a five-brigades operation and involved the largest Soviet contingent of para troops committed to combat in the post-World War II era. In addition to Soviet forces, 6,000 Afghan Army troops from their 8th and 20th and the 38 Commando Brigade took part along with local militias. This brings the tally of troops to over 30,000 which make it a major corps sized operation. The operation commenced with massive air strikes by 36 TU-36 Badger bombers and scores of SU-24 fighter bombers. An airborne command post was established in an AN-12 aircraft. Representatives from the General Staff in Moscow oversaw this operation. The preparations were too massive to conceal. Masood got wind of the operation and quickly evacuated the Panjshir valley floor and climbed to the heights. He launched a spoiling attack on the troops assembling near Anawa.

The KGB had planned to assassinate Masood, but the plan failed as a key double agent defected. On 21 April 1984, the massive Soviet operation commenced with air strikes, but bad weather restricted their usefulness. The Soviets now unveiled their new tactics of inserting stop groups (or Anvils) using heli-borne or para troops. These established blocks on the heights before the mechanized ground assault began. The tanks and BMPs trundled into the Panjshir valley and by 24 April reached their intermediate objectives at Rekha and Khanji.

In Phase II of the operation Soviet heli-borne battalions were launched to seize Dashit-e-Rawar and the entrance to the main Panjshir valley (The Taliban was forced to recoil from here later in 1996). The fiercest battle of the Afghan War took place here. One Soviet heli-borne battalion moved out of artillery range and suffered heavy casualties as the guerrillas began to close in on it. It called in air strike to save itself. On 02 May 1984 the Soviet bombers caught a large group of Mujahideen moving in the open and inflicted very heavy casualties.

The Soviets now applied the tactic of having separate columns converge on a given objective from many directions while heli-borne forces were launched inside the cordon. Soviet mechanized columns also moved into the parallel valleys of the Anderab river. A Soviet column took off from Khinjan near Salang tunnel and pushed into the Anderab valley to link up with heli-borne forces. Other Soviet forces moved out from Jalalabad and secured Alishay and Kantiwar passes, the southern approaches to the Panjshir. Masood desperately tried to break contact and avoid battle. Air power, however, proved of limited utility in the narrow river valleys. This was Masood's saving grace and he survived. Afghan militia forces moved down the Anjuman valley to secure the area and establish forts. The Soviets suffered 500 casualties. The operation failed to annihilate Masood's Tajik guerilla bands but removed the threat to the Soviet lines of communication. As Masood fought alone, guerillas from other areas tried to help him by activating their sectors. One group came from Wardek for reinforcements.

In September 1996, during the war with the Taliban, Masood vacated Kabul and retreated to the Panjshir valley, where he gave a bloody nose to the Taliban. Getting Masood and his Tajiks out of the Panjshir would take a corps sized offensive to be meaningful.

1985

The Kunar Offensive: In May 1985, the Soviets launched a major offensive to relieve the besieged garrison of Barikot. The Jalalabad based 1 Corps took part. The operation was spearheaded by the 9th and 11th Afghan Infantry divisions along with 38 and 57 Commando brigades and two infantry regiments from other divisions, the Soviet Motor Rifle Regiment, one Spetsnatz (Special Forces) regiment and one airborne regiment. This was the first mammoth operation by the resuscitated Afghan army.

This resulted in heavy fighting. Over 150 combat air sorties were flown per day. The intensity of the fighting can be gauged from the fact that one Hero of the Soviet Union (the highest gallantry award) was given in this campaign. A Soviet para battalion was heli-lifted inside Barikot. It then broke out to link with the advancing forces. The siege of Barikot was thus lifted. However as soon as the Soviets withdrew, the Mujahideen, who had fled re-entered.

In June 1985, Soviet Gen Mikhail M. Zaitsev was appointed as the Southern TVD Commander and given two years to deliver a military solution.

Second Paktia Offensive: This was launched in August 1985 near Herat. Its aim was to destroy the large Mujahideen strongholds in Azru, Jadji, Chamkani and Khost. It also sought to relieve the siege of Ali Khel in the Paktia province and interdict the infiltration and supply routes from Pakistan. The increasing shift in operational responsibility to the Afghanistan Army was again evident from the line-up of forces for this attack. From the Soviet side, 15,000 troops included three Motor Rifle Regiments along with Air Assault, Spetsnaz and reconnaissance troops:

from the Afghan Army, the 3rd Corps with 11, 12 and 25 Infantry Divisions along with 37 and 38 Commando Brigades and other brigades from 7 and 8 Infantry Divisions took part.

Families of Mujahideen were massacred at Loggar, Khurd and Azra. This forced the Mujahideen to pause and evacuate their families to Pakistan. Para battalions were air-landed inside the besieged garrison of Khost and Ali Khel. They broke out to join the relieving columns in a repeat of the tactics of fighting break out.

The combined Soviet-Afghan Army offensive made rapid progress. Jalaluddin Haqqani was the Mujahideen leader in Pakistan. A major showcase base at Zhawar had been built near the Afghan border by the Mujahideen. The Soviet-Afghan Army offensive now aimed at Zhawar. Heavy fighting took place there, with the Mujahideen fighting fiercely in defence. The offensive finally wore down just one kilometer short of Zhawar by September 1985.The Afghan Mujahideen had received 107 mm rocket launchers from the Americans and the Chinese and started sneak rocket attacks on Kabul from end 1985. This led the Soviets to undertake a major effort to strengthen Kabul defenses. Three lines of outposts were established for perimeter defence and by 1987 Kabul was secure. KHAD, the official Afghan security agency, now displayed considerable improvement and efficiency.

1986

In winter 1985-86 the Soviet KGB tried to spark off a transporter uprising of the Pathan tribes. It tried to get the Shinwari and Mohmand tribes to rebel against Pakistan and cut supply lines on both sides of the border. In conjunction, Afghan government troops launched another corps-sized offensive that destroyed the Zhawar base of Jalaluddin Haqqani. Afghan Army forces also launched offensives around Herat and Nazim Valley in Nangrahar province. Soviet forces attacked the Faryab province.

To counter Soviet air superiority a large number of SAM-7 missiles were given to the Mujahideen by the Americans and Chinese. Operations in Logar valley saw the mass use of these SAM-7s. The Soviet tactics now shifted to mass use of Soviet Spetsnaz (Special Forces) to lay ambushes and interdict the Mujahideen supply lines. Soviet interdiction efforts around Kandahar were particularly effective.

Soviet President Mikhail Gorbachev had by now begun his drive for Perestroika and Glasnost reforms. The Afghan War was a heavy economic drain. The Soviet economy was hovering on the brink of collapse. Gorbachev was keen to terminate the Afghan operation as quickly as possible. Babrak Karmal was replaced with the KHAD chief Najibullah. The search for a compromise commenced. Najibullah called for a pro-Communist Loya Jirga (tribal council) in 1986. Gorbachev gave his "Bleeding Wound" speech in Moscow.

The Soviets, meanwhile, seemed to have completed the reconstruction of the Afghan Army. Two corps-sized offensives by the Afghan Army in 1985 and 1986 convinced them that it could stand alone. They felt they had stabilized the situation adequately to contemplate withdrawal. The Americans had by now introduced the Stinger missile to counter the Soviet air assault tactics. On 26 September 1986 the Stingers reportedly brought down four Soviet helicopters in Nangrahar. But the impact of the Stingers seems overrated, as is borne out by the fact that the Afghan Army held out for four years after the Soviet pull-out in 1989.

1987

The Soviets started winding down military operations and began to seek a political solution. Najibullah declared a unilateral cease-fire and called for national reconciliation. To pressurize Pakistan the Soviets began air raids across the border. One Soviet aircraft and one F-16 were shot down in these incursions. Pakistan exploited this opportunity to the fullest to seek AWACS, F-16s and other American arms aid.

The Afghan Mujahideen now started sneak 107mm rocket attacks on Soviet posts and Kandahar city itself. The Afghan Army launched a major retaliatory attack on Arghandab with 15 Infantry Division and a tank brigade. The operations were controlled by the Afghan minister for defense and interior and led to heavy fighting. The Jowjani Militia under the KGB trained Gen Abdul Rashid Dostam fought well in these encounters.

Paktia Offensive: Soviet Special Forces again launched an offensive into Paktia to relieve the besieged garrisons at Ali Sher and Jadji and press on to the Pakistan border. Stingers were used extensively. As a result the Soviets reduced the use of helicopters and relied more on BM-21 Grad Rocket Launchers for saturation fire. Extensive mines were laid to seal the border. Masood, the most successful guerilla leader, now began to raise central forces that could operate outside their native areas. He attacked Khalafghan garrison in Takhar province. The raid was highly successful but due to jealousy the Hekmatyar-led Pashtun Mujahideen proved most unhelpful in this operation. Stingers were claimed to have inflicted 68 per cent kill rates in 1987 and brought down 150-200 aircraft/helicopters.

1988

Diplomatic initiatives were intensified. New emphasis was placed on the Geneva negotiations process. The KGB and KHAD infiltrated the Mujahideen ranks and blew up the Mujahideen ammunition dump run by the ISI at Ohjri in Pakistan. The KGB launched a very highly successful psychological warfare campaign to exacerbate tensions between the Mujahideen field commanders fighting inside Afghanistan and the Pakistan supported political leaders ensconced in the comfortable bungalows of Peshawar. The Pakistan based seven parties tried to form a Mujahideen interim government-in-exile. Pakistan was now worried about the eventual return of the Afghan refugees.

Relief of Khost: In October 1987 the resistance forces besieged the Khost garrison once more. A very major relief operation with the Afghan 7, 8 and 12 Infantry Divisions and 20,000 strong Soviet force from the 103 Guards Airborne Division the 108 Motorized Rifle Division and special operations brigade was launched. The Afghan Army led the attacks while the Soviets remained in the rear in an overmatch role to test the efficacy of the rebuilt Afghan Army. Massed artillery was employed (especially 152 mm guns firing beehive rounds at close ranges and BM-22 multi-barrel rocket launchers). The Soviets flew in an air-borne brigade at night to link up with the garrison and launch break-out attacks. The resistance leader Haqqani was wounded and the Mujahideen withdrew. By 30 December 1988 Khost was relieved.

In the same year President Zia ul Haq of Pakistan was killed in an air crash. Zia ul Haq was the main backer of Hekmatyar who was by now thoroughly unpopular. The Pakistanis had deliberately marginalised the field commanders amongst the Mujahideen to prevent any nationalist Afghan forces from coming up. They wanted to conquer Afghanistan by proxy through quislings and clients like Hekmatyar, who had no actual following inside Afghanistan.

David C. Isby writes, "Throughout their battlefield involvement *the limited Soviet contingent of forces in Afghanistan stressed a relatively low level of operational commitment and rate of casualties, consistent with the attainment of a long-term solution that emphasized the political rather than the military aspect of war.*" This reduced the options for large-scale escalation. Soviet low-intensity operations however did not mean low technology. The most modern weapons in the Soviet arsenal were used and tested. The Soviets used large-scale bombing to destroy rural agriculture and punish offending tribes. They depopulated locals from areas around highways and infiltration routes. The campaign resulted in heavy civilian casualties varyingly estimated at 600,000 875,000 (1.2 million by Gallup organization). The cost was estimated at $ 4-8 million per day and $ 50 billion in total. It was to cut their cost that the Soviets rebuilt the Afghan army, tested it from 1984 to 1987 and withdrew in 1989 when they were confident that it could stand alone. It stood alone for three years after the Soviet withdrawal but collapsed when the Russians stopped economic aid and military supplies. Problems came when Najibullah's rentier regime began to default on payments to its troops. The collapse of the Najibullah regime therefore conforms to the pattern of rentier state formation and collapse once the external resources are withdrawn. It also saw a virtual partition of Afghanistan along ethnic fault lines. The Pashtuns declined in historical terms even as the Farsiwan (the Tajiks, Uzbeks and Hazaras) rose at their expense.

A detailed and exhaustive analysis of Soviet operations in Afghanistan has been carried out simply because these provide the most recent and relevant military models for the ongoing US/NATO operations in Afghanistan and provide operational benchmarks against which one can test ongoing operations and theories/hypotheses. To make informed judgments about ongoing operations, the only objective way is to compare them to earlier operations in the same geographical and social context. That is the prime value of the study of military history.

REFERENCES

1. David C. Isby, *War in a Distant Country: Afghanistan Invasion and Resistance,* Arms and Armour Press, London, 1989. Most operational details in the present volume have been collated from this source.
2. Anthony Cordesman, *Lessons of Modern War, volume III, Afghanistan,* Brassy and Bergemon, London, 1990. Cordesman's analysis of military operations in Afghanistan is the most comprehensive one to date.
3. Gen (retd) Mohd Yahaya Navroj and Lt Col Lester W. Grau, *The Soviet Experience in Afghanistan,* Military Review, September-October 1995.
4. *Ibid.*
5. Barnett R. Rubin, *The Fragmentation of Afghanistan,* Yale University Press, p.125.
6. *Ibid.*
7. Seth S Jones, *Counter Insurgency in Afghanistan,* Rand Corporation, National Defence Research Institute, Santa Monica, USA 2008.
8. Elizabeth Gould and Paul Fitzgerald, *Invisible History: Afghanistan's Untold Story* Brassey and Bergemon, London, 2008.
9. Steve Coll, *Ghost Wars: The Secret History of the CIA, Afghanistan and Bin Laden, From the Soviet Invasion to Sep 10, 2001.* Penguin Books, London, 2004.

3

Analysing the Taliban Phenomenon: The Current State of Insurgency in Afghanistan

INTRODUCTION: THE TALIBAN

In the fall of 1989, the ISI started a programme to raise a conventional Mujahideen Army of eight battalions under its protégé Hekmatyar. This was grandiosely called the *Army of Sacrifice* (Laskar-i-Isar). In spring 1990 this army had fielded some six thousand soldiers south of Kabul. Hekmatyar got a significant opening when he secretly negotiated an alliance with the Durrani Pashtuns of the Khalq faction in Kabul.

On 7 March 1990, General Shah Nawaz Tanai launched a coup in Kabul. ISI and Saudi intelligence agencies, says Rubin, paid upto US$150,000 each to other Mujahideen leaders to join the coup. But the coup failed and Tanai fled to Pakistan. There Hekmatyar appointed him the commander of the *Army of Sacrifice*.

On 6 August 1990, the ISI again tried to Co-ordinate a massive assault on Kabul by Hekmatyar. Rubin states that over 40,000 rockets and 700 truckloads of ammunition were supplied to Hekmatyar by the Pakistanis. This shower of rockets and the assault itself would have caused thousands of civilian casualties in Kabul. As per Rubin, the US State Department forcefully intervened to stop this assault. The US realized the Islamist game plan of ISI and told it forcefully to drop Hekmatyar and Sayyaf. The US began to aid some independent-minded Mujahideen commanders inside Afghanistan. A National Commanders' Shura was held inside Afghanistan in October 1990. The ISI's new Director General, Assad Durrani, insisted on attending this Shura but was not allowed to participate. In March 1991, writes Rubin, the USA and the ISI again threw in their resources into the battle for the capture of Khost town in Paktika province. The Afghan government garrison fell to the force of Haqqani, a local military leader.

The cynical alliances between Hekmatyar and former Khalq military commanders led to widespread disillusionment amongst the Afghan Mujahideen. Many mujahideen leaders now sought autonomy from the ISI. *One way to gain financial freedom from the purse-strings of the ISI was by taking to the cultivation of poppy in a big way. Hekmatyar went even further. He began to establish factories for the processing of opium into heroin in partnership with Pakistan's heroin syndicates.*

Despite the media hype, there never was a clear-cut Mujahideen victory in Afghanistan. The PDPA fell essentially because of a serious ethnic divide between Pashtuns and the Farsiwans (the Tajiks, Uzbeks and Hazaras). The most significant role in these events was played not even by Ahmed Shah Masood (the famed lion of Panjshir) but by Abdul Rashid Dostam and his 65,000 strong Uzbek militia (Jowzjani militia).

The Uzbeks and Tajiks have proved to be inherently more amenable to military discipline and service in organized and large military units. The Pashtun tribes have proved too prone to internecine clashes and personal adjustment problems in regular military service. The Pashtun is an excellent guerilla fighter but possibly too much of an individualist. His recent skills at regular conventional warfare have not been very impressive.

Najibullah was firmly in saddle till end-1991. His problems started with US-USSR agreement in end-1991 to suspend all military aid to their Afghan clients. This hurt Najibullah most, as Pakistan's ISI and Saudi Arabia freely continued their aid to the Mujahideen. Najibullah now found it difficult to keep paying Dostam's Uzbek militia.

The Parcham factions of Babrak Karmal had earlier concluded that it was the Pashtuns who were primarily supportive of Mujahideen. To counterbalance them they had encouraged and armed the non-Pashtun minorities. This overturned the historical power equations within Afghanistan. The Parchamites brought about a radical change in this inter-tribal equation by arming the Uzbeks and Tajiks in a big way.

The failed coup of Pashtun General Shah Nawaz Tanai forced Najibullah to rely further on the non-Pashtuns. By end-91 however, he realized that this Pashtun-Farsiwan cleavage had gone too far and could even lead to an ethnic division of the country. A Pashtun himself, Najibullah tried to trim the power of the non-Pashtuns. His Pashtun leanings soon became evident and the country became sharply polarized on ethnic lines. Najibullah stopped paying Dostam's Uzbek militia, which promptly mutinied. The Tajik General Momin had started cooperating with Masood, a fellow Tajik. Najibullah was greatly demoralized as he saw the looming ethnic partition of the country. He had been in touch with the UN. Sevan, the UN representative had been putting much pressure on him to step down peacefully and hand over power to the mujahideen. He had offered to hand over power to King Zahir Shah or a neutral force.

Najibullah was however, overtaken by events .The Farsiwans became aware of his perceived "sell-out" to the UN. They resented the UN bodies' attempt to reimpose Pashtun domination over Afghanistan by installing a bunch of Pashtun political leaders who had largely spent the war in the cosy comforts of Peshawar.

On 8 March 1992, in a radio broadcast from Kabul, Najibullah announced his readiness to step down. On 19 March 1992 itself, a coalition of Parcham forces and Northern rebels seized Mazar-e-Sharif. Dostam struck viciously and defeated the Khalq 18th Division led by General Rasul in Balkh. With the collaboration of Parcham troops, Masood's forces took over the Bagram air base. Dostam's 65,000-men Uzbek militia now swept south and took control of the whole area between Mazar-e-Sharif and Kabul. They invited Masood and his Tajik militia to come into Kabul. The state of Afghanistan had frankly come apart at its ethnic seams. The Khalq-Pashtun factions of Najibullah forces were alarmed. They in turn got in touch with Hekmatyar and asked him to come in before it was too late.

On 25 April 1992, the forces of Dostam and Masood entered Kabul city, expelled the Khalq Pashtun forces and took control of Kabul. It was hardly a Mujahideen victory. Pakistan made a great show of triumphalism. The then Pakistani Prime Minister Nawaz Sharif and his ISI strongman Lt. Gen. Hamid Gul entered Kabul like some sort of conquering heroes. In the Pakistani press, there was a strident chorus to simply ingest Afghanistan and gain strategic space and depth against arch rival India. Afghan-Pakistan relations deteriorated rapidly and sharply in 1993-94. The Pakistani Embassy in Kabul was ransacked.

In effect, Afghanistan had been virtually partitioned over ethnic faultlines. Whereas the non-Pashtuns had consolidated a military alliance, the Pashtun themselves were badly divided into seven squabbling factions. Pakistan backed its protégé Hekmatyar and hoped that he would assume control. Pakistan then cobbled together on 01 January 1994, an alliance of convenience between Dostam and Hekmatyar. Hekmatyar, however, failed miserably to take Kabul. Rabbani stayed firm in his post and the Tajik forces led by Masood and ex-government troops under the command of Gen Abdul Wahid Babajan (COS from 1980 to 1984 and last military chief under Najibullah) effectively checkmated the Pashtuns of Hekmatyar in battle.

THE RISE OF THE TALIBAN

Pakistan was now forced to reappraise its policy. The CIA, which found Hekmatyar and his support to Arab and trans-national Islamic fundamentalism quite unpalatable, pressurised the ISI to dump Hekmatyar. Benazir Bhutto had assumed power in Islamabad. Keen to ease the ISI-military stranglehold on Pakistan's Afghan policy, she appointed Maj Gen Nasirullah Babar (Retd) as her Interior Minister. Babar had been her father's adviser on Afghan affairs as far back as 1974-75 and had been instrumental in recruiting all the first-generation Afghan Mujahideen leaders (including Mohammed Omar).

In 1993, Babar hit upon the idea of recruiting a new force from the Islamic *madrasas* on the Afghan-Pakistan borders. Saudi Arabia had provided enormous funds for establishing these madrasas; more than 2,512 had been opened in Pakistan's West Punjab province alone. Mullah Omar, a onetime protégé of General Babar was chosen as the new leader to replace the discredited Hekmatyar and Sayyaf group.

Fazlur Rahman's Role: The Taliban's principal supporter was Fazlur Rahman, the Jammat-i-Ulema-Islam (JUI) leader from Baluchistan. The first batch of Talibs from seminaries run by Maulana Fazlur Rahman was trained by the Frontier Constabulary Corps and the Sibi Scouts in training camps near Baluch border with Afghanistan. The Taliban started with a modest strength of some 2,500. It came to light initially when it rescued a Pakistani convoy from a local Mujahideen warlord. It then captured Doorahi, a small town on the outskirts of Kandahar. The Taliban then attacked and captured Spin Boldak. At this juncture, the Taliban seems to have suddenly become an alternative option for Pakistan. The ISI, which seems to have despaired with Hekmatyar, switched support to the Taliban. Mullah Omar was certainly a more charismatic military leader with a better fighting record than Hekmatyar. Omar had been studying in the Jamat-ul-Uloom-i-Islamiya Madrasa of Karachi. The bulk of the Taliban leadership is from this seminary (three of the six-member council).

The Taliban was now rapidly built up from a nondescript force of 2,500 to 30,000. The ISI touted it as the force that could unify and deliver all Afghanistan. The proposal received extensive support from Saudi Arabia and the consortium of oil companies (led by UNOCAL) that were keen to establish oil and natural gas pipelines from Turkmenistan to Karachi via Afghanistan. Saudi money and Pakistani military equipment and support poured in. Reportedly the Taliban was then getting over US$70million a month for its upkeep. Its strength had swelled up to 50,000. It had 300 tanks and APCs and a squadron of MiG aircraft.

In November 1994, the Taliban captured Kandahar. It attacked Hekmatyar and ejected him from his strongholds in south Kabul. The ISI poured in money to buy off the Mujahideen opposition. By September 1995, the Taliban had captured Herat and then Herat-Kandahar-Quetta route. The Taliban failed to take Kabul in 1995. By 1996 it had managed to purchase most of the local commanders of Hekmatyar. It captured Jalalabad in August 1996 and in a rapid blitz captured Kabul without any serious opposition.

The Tajiks led by Rabbani and Masood had been supporting Tajik Islamic opposition groups in Tajikistan. To neutralize their clout, Russia and the Central Asian states pressurised the Uzbek warlord Dostam to act against Masood. Unable to withstand the joint pressure, Masood in a far-sighted tactical gambit, vacated Kabul and withdrew to his Panjshir redoubt.

By 1997, the Taliban had bought off Bashir Salangi and paid a bribe of US$200 million to Maj Gen Abdul Malik Pehelwan, one of Dostam's disgruntled Generals. In April 1997, having purchased most of Dostam's Generals, Taliban marched into Mazar-e-Sharif in triumph, but its triumph was short-lived. Their display of terror infuriated the Shia and Uzbek population, which rose in spontaneous revolt and slaughtered the Taliban. Mullah Mohammed Ghaus, the Taliban's foreign minister and a large number of its senior leaders were killed or captured. At this stage the Tajiks, Uzbeks and Hazaras counter-attacked jointly. They recaptured the Salang tunnel, freed Mazar-e-Sharif and came within gun range of Kabul. The next year however, the Taliban received extensive support from Saudi Arabia and the ISI. Some 11,000 Pakistani Pathan troops in mufti now joined it to operate the tanks, artillery and aircrafts. This tilted the scales decisively and the Taliban captured Mazar-e-Shrief and Herat. These were two critical Air bases for the supply of the Northern Alliance forces. The Taliban once again carried out large scale massacres of the Uzbeks and Hazaras. This ethnic cleansing almost sparked off a war with Iran which massed over 250,000 troops on the Afghan borders. Till this juncture the American Oil Company UNOCOL was enthusiastically supporting the Taliban. It was then that Osama Bin Laden struck the US embassies in Kenya and Tanzania and the US was forced to respond with Cruise Missile strikes on the bases of Bin Laden in Afghanistan. 9/11 followed and the rest is very familiar history. It was one of the worst instances of "Blow-back" in covert operations. The US was forced to launch Op Enduring Freedom to topple the Taliban.

OVERALL STATE OF MILITANCY

The current level of the insurgency in Afghanistan can be attributed to two episodes of historical hubris. In 2001, Mullah Omar's Taliban decided very foolishly indeed to fight like a regular army and defend cities and towns in set piece battles. It presented concentrated targets which were destroyed with ridiculous ease by the US Air force. The Northern Alliance simply mopped up in the wake of the Air offensive. The surprising ease of the victory over the Taliban in turn now generated a *very high level of hubris in the Pentagon. Some patently wrong lessons were learnt from this campaign which flew in the face of the accumulated wisdom of conventional Military History.* Conquest and control of the ground can only be accomplished by putting sufficient number of "Boots on the ground."However downsizing and Airpower had become the new Pentagon dogma. After major combat ended in Afghanistan, Lt Gen Tommy Franks argued that *America's combat footprint in Afghanistan had to be small, both for military and geopolitical reasons. He envisaged that an American force of just 10,000 backed by robust Air- Power within the country,* was adequate to hold Afghanistan. This was a most highly flawed force to space ratio that allowed the Taliban not just to escape to sanctuaries in FATA and NWFP in Pakistan but later regroup and stage a significant comeback. This was natural as

- There was no Afghan National Army to secure the Afghan population centres and communications or even seal the porous border with Pakistan.
- This forced the Americans to rely upon the already discredited War Lords to secure the country. After the Soviet withdrawal these warlords had let loose a reign of terror and lawlessness. The people of Afghanistan were so fed up of the depredations of these warlords that they had initially welcomed the Taliban with relief in the hope that they would restore the rule of law and bring peace to Afghanistan. The Taliban's fanaticism however, had become another nightmare for the Afghan citizens.
- However bringing back the discredited warlords by the Americans in effect discredited the Central Government of President Karzai and undercut its authority. The warlords and erstwhile Mujahideen Commanders were reinserted in positions of authority and subsequently acquired domination over most of the political institutions The warlords corrupt and arbitrary behaviour soon *alienated the Afghan people and evaporated the fund of goodwill that was so apparently visible in the wake of the overthrow of the Taliban.*
- The US and its Allies took inordinately long to raise a viable Afghan Army that would unify and make the Afghan state governable. By 2011 the ANA is supposed to reach its final size of 134,000.This is highly inadequate for a country the size and ruggedness of

Afghanistan. It merits recalling that the pre- Soviet era Afghan Army was 350,000 strong and the Afghan Army recreated by the Soviets before they left was 550,000 strong. This was a viable force size for stabilizing Afghanistan and had held the Mujahideen at bay for three years.

- *"The light military footprint post Op Enduring Freedom,* writes Thomas Ruttig, *created the operational space and bad governance that provided the moral space for a return of the Taliban."* A revived and rested Taliban now found the border undefended and the bulk of Afghanistan without any military presence. It simply seeped in and revived its insurgency. Some 10,000 Taliban with about 1000 Uzbek fighters, and 500 of Osama's Arabs now began to destabilize the Afghan state. On the Pakistan side they were backed by some 20,000 Pakistani Taliban-(Tehrik-e-Taliban Pakistan, Tehrik-e-Nifaze Shariat-e-Mohammad-TNSM and other groups and criminal elements). Not only was the Force to Space ratio terribly lopsided, even the Insurgent to Security Forces ratio was badly skewed. The Americans are now paying for almost *a decade of serious under-resourcing and underfunding of the Afghan war.* The surge may be too little too late.
- The key problem was the American reluctance to put troops on the ground. This led to their over-reliance on the discredited warlords. Of the first group of 32 provincial governors appointed in 2002, at least 25 were former warlords/militia commanders. Smaller warlords provided the bulk of district governors. It is noteworthy that the Afghan population was thoroughly fed up of the constant internecine fighting and corruption of these Pakistan supported Mujahideen commanders of the post-Soviet era. A rapid raising of a viable ANA would have greatly reduced the power of the warlords and in fact greatly reduced significant costs for the USA in terms of deploying American forces. However, this was tragically not done. During 2002-06 the Taliban simply seeped back. In fact, a major recruitment drive was launched in September 2002 inside Pakistan and Afghanistan. Slowly, groups as large as 80 to 150 strong started making inroads into the Southern provinces of Afghanistan bordering FATA & NWFP.

SPREAD OF INSURGENCY

- **2002.** From bases in NWFP & FATA the insurgents began to creep into the fringes of the Southern Afghan provinces of Paktia, Paktika, Kandahar, Helmand and Nimroz.
- **2003.** The Taliban made inroads into Kunar, Zabul and Ghazni provinces in the south as also Badghiz province in the north during this period.
- **2004.** Taliban insurgents began operations in Uruzgan.
- **2005-06.** the most significant surge in Taliban activity occurred in 2005-06. Pakistan was now convinced that the USA/NATO simply lacked the stomach to stay the course in Afghanistan. The ISI's Afghan Bureau now started providing significant help. The Taliban insurgency made deep inroads into Nimroz, Helmand, Farah, Uruzgan, Ghazni, Wardak and Kapisa provinces. They were now operating in bands that were 300-400 strong. This was the major turning point of the insurgency.

There are currently three clear tiers of Taliban:

- *First Tier: Quetta Shura* led by Mullah Omar was based in Quetta and has now reportedly shifted to the Binori Mosque Madrasa in Karachi. It is active in Helmand and Kandahar.
- *Second Tier: Haqqani Shura,* considered a strategic asset of the ISI, is led by Jalaluddin Haqqani, a former Mujahideen commander. Operates in Khost, Logar, Paktia and Paktika. It is based in Waziristan.
- *Third Tier: The Hizb-e-Islami Shura* based in NWFP is led by Gulbuddin Hekmatyar, former Mujahideen commander and asset of ISI. Operates in Waziristan, Kunar, Laghman, Nangrahar, etc.
- *Local Cadres:* The bulk of the IED, stand off fire attacks and rockets are fired by locally recruited cadres who are paid by the Taliban from its corpus of Narcotics profits and extortion of aid agencies operating in Afghanistan. Only 30% of the Taliban are full time cadres. The balance are all local recruits.

The UN Secretary General in a report to the Security Council in June 2009 indicated the rising trend in violence in Afghanistan thus,

"The overall number of security incidents continued to rise during the reporting period, [March to May 2009] with May figures exceeding 1,000 for the first time since 2001." He also indicated that 2009 saw a 43 per cent increase in the monthly average number of security incidents, from 519 in the first four months of 2008 to 740 during the same period in 2009. The UN Secretary General also reported that there has been an increase in foreign fighters, most likely affiliated with Al-Qaida, engaged alongside the Taliban. The recent presidential elections saw a wave of suicide bombings and terrorist attacks to intimidate the voters. However despite this there was 40-50% voter turnout.

Key Markers of Increased Violence

Number of security incidents - Overall monthly Average in 2009 till May - 43 percent increase.	519 in first four months of 2008. 740 in first four months of 2009.	May 2009 First time incident figure crossed 1000 in a month

[Source: UN Security Council Report].

The impact of the fighting on security and safety of the citizens was highlighted by thc UN Secretary General with the Taliban deliberately targeting government officials, employees, religious scholars, civilian contractors of the Government and the aid community. In 2009 he indicated a general rise in assassinations, abductions, incidents of intimidation and the direct targeting of aid workers, though only one aid worker was killed during the reporting period.

- The International Security Assistance Force (ISAF) and the Afghan National Army is making some progress. This may not be satisfactory under the circumstances with problems of corruption and lack of permeation of central authority to the periphery of the government marring the current ability for governance and thus winning over the people. However the US surge and change of rules of engagement with the people as the centre of gravity has shown better response from the grass roots. However, a fair assessment will take some more time. The reduction of air strikes is also a major advantage gained in the recent past. The restricted combat commitment of some of the coalition forces in Afghanistan is however a matter of concern.

- *The US Surge.* In effect, the US Surge sought to put on ground some 17,000 additional troops and 4000 trainers. The combat component had largely come in (to sanitise the Southern and Eastern provinces before the Presidential elections). The US formations involved in the Surge are:
- *82nd Combat Aviation Brigade.* This has deployed some 100 helicopters at Kandahar and another 30 at Uruzgan. It has some 4000 troops. Its initial operations are said to have been fairly successful but the casualties have risen significantly.
- *2nd Marine Expeditionary Force.* This has some 8000 troops.
- *5th Striker Brigade.* This has 4000 troops. In itself these formations constitute a long overdue accretion of force levels. However the accretion is not very significant in purely quantitative terms and unless this is enhanced, may amount to too little too late. Major operations have been launched in the key opium growing province of Helmand in 2008 & 2009. The US and British forces have taken fairly heavy casualties.
- Major offensives were launched in the month of July 2009. The British launched Op Panther Claw in the Helmand river valley. The 19th Light Brigade was employed in this operation, which was completed on 27 July 09. The British suffered inordinately high casualties of 27 killed and 57 wounded. 50% to 60% of the casualties however were non-battle injuries like heat stroke. The British had to fly in 125 troops as reinforcements, and the 19th Light Brigade will be relieved by the 11th Light Brigade. The total number of British casualties in Afghanistan has now exceeded those that they suffered in Iraq. There has been considerable concern in the British media over the rising casualties. The US Marine Corps task force launched Op Strike and Op Sword. They suffered a casualty count of 14 killed in this operation. Around 300 German troops along with a battalion of the ANA launched operations in the north.
- The overall strength of the US troops in Afghanistan currently is 68,000. The NATO/ISAF forces have provided another 32,000

troops. Even this contingent is proving to be highly inadequate. Till the US surge most of these were confined to their bases and relied upon airpower to protect themselves. This caused considerable collateral damage and has alienated the population. Gen David Petraeus of the US Central Command and Lt Gen Stanley McChrystal want to revert to the classical COIN (Counter Insurgency) strategy of Clear, Hold, Build. This strategy places emphasis on protecting the population. For this Gen McChrystal has asked for 40,000 60,000 additional US troops and a doubling of the ANA/Afghan Police. In actual fact, this is a conservative estimate that is still on the low side. Unfortunately, the US and its European allies are shaken by the initial casualties caused by the surge. Much will depend on public opinion back home, and the political willingness to absorb casualties. This appears rather doubtful. US Vice President Joe Biden has put forth an alternative Counter Terrorism Strategy (as opposed to COIN) that focuses simply on the Al Qaeda and not the Taliban. It seeks to thin out US military presence on the ground and rely solely upon US airpower, Predator strikes and Special Forces to inflict casualties. However, this has worked to an extent in NWFP & FATA only in conjunction with major ground operations launched by the Pak Army. On their own there is very little chance of these succeeding in Afghanistan. The classical COIN solution offered by Gen McChrystal is more likely to succeed provided the US shows the stamina and resolve to stay the course for at least one to two decades.

At the same time the Taliban is largely intact and active. It is split in various groups—Quetta Shura, Southern and Northern Command, Haqqani Network, Hizb e Islami and networked with drug and criminal gangs, supported by the Tehreek-e-Taliban Pakistan or TTP and the Pakistani establishment. There are however serrations within, especially between the local and central leadership. The main tactics are that of IEDs which is proving highly effective. It has also developed the capacity for complex terrorist attacks combining two or three suicide bombers with fire assault by a number of fighters in Kabul and other regional headquarters. Only 30% of the Taliban are full time cadres. The bulk of them are locally recruited for individual acts like planting IEDs, or direct fire assaults or firing rockets. They are well paid by the Taliban who earn handsome revenues from the Opium trade, and extortion from the Aid agencies and NGOs working for the reconstruction of Afghanistan.

Pakistan has under taken counter militancy operations in the Malakand Agency including Swat, Buner and Dir which has ostensibaly swept away the Taliban. The second phase has already commenced in South Waziristan. The operations have been certified by the Americans as effective but there are many caveats. Some three million tribal people have been forced to flee their homes and are now living in Refugee camps. This is bound to generate a great deal of resentment in the tribal population. The complex counter militancy strategy kinetic operations, targeting leadership, tribal militias, peace deals and local agreements being followed does not create confidence of success. Attacks on NATO/ISAF convoys in Malakand are continuing. Thus on the whole the commitment of the Pakistan government and the army is highly suspect.The recent Pakistani operations are more in the nature of offensive sweeps which can have only a temporary neutralization effect. Lasting neutralization would require the Pakistani Army to hold a classical CI Grid or follow what the Americans term the "*Clear, Hold, Build* "model. This it seems most unwilling to do. Its operations in Swat were in relatively open and plains terrain of the valley where it was able to use heavy firepower, airpower and tanks to overawe the tribals. However, the bulk of the Taliban cadres have simply melted away into the hills and have survived to fight again. To be really effective Pakistan will have to deploy a permanent CI grid for minimum upto one to two decades in these areas. It is extremely doubtful if the Pakistan Army is willing to commit these force levels for such extended durations. What is even more critical is the ethnic composition of the Pakistan Army itself. 28% of its rank and file is of Pashtun origin and their loyalty has already been seriously stretched by the ongoing GWOT which requires them to fight their own kith and kin. The heavy collateral damage caused by extensive use of airpower and artillery in these areas and large scale outflow of refugees are further complicating the issue and could lead to a serious undermining of the institution of the Army itself.

Given this complex operational flux, the violence in Afghanistan is likely to continue in the months ahead and sustained commitment of the security forces would be necessary. A detailed analysis of various issues is given in the succeeding paragraphs.

THE TALIBAN: AN OVERVIEW

It is tempting, says Antonio Giustozzi, to see the Taliban as an expression of the rural-urban conflict in Afghanistan. However, it is important to stress that they were expressions of a specific rural culture, that of village Mullahs, and stood in opposition to the tribal codex of Pashtunwali (and the traditional hierarchy of Sardars and tribal leaders). The neo-Taliban have absorbed from the foreign Jehadist allies, a more flexible and less orthodox attitude towards imported technologies and techniques (They are now producing propaganda tapes and videos, and making extensive use of IEDs). This ideology now has a free market orientation. They have been outsourcing and paying local tribes/fighters for specific works like laying IEDs and standoff firings on US/NATO troops and aircrafts. The arms/ammunitions are largely supplied by the ISI or purchased from the Darra Adam Khel arms bazaar of NWFP as also from Northern Afghanistan. Pakistan has strong influence in Southern Afghanistan as all trade is conducted in Pakistani Rupee and the tribes across the Durand Line are closely inter-related. Above all there is a strong perception that while the USA and NATO are likely to exit, Pakistan will remain a force to reckon with.

The Taliban who were in power in Afghanistan between 1996 and 2001 are a fundamentalist Sunni group espousing the Deobandi ideology which grew out of the post Soviet withdrawal anarchy in Afghanistan after 1989. The group primarily comprises Pashtun based in the South East of the country which form over 40 percent of the Afghan population as the largest ethnic group.(However they do not constitute a majority.) The ethnic linkages across the Durand Line denote that the Pasthuns have a strong base of support in Pakistan's tribal areas (which do not have the presence of the government) going back to the British era of exclusion. Most of South Asia's tribal areas are currently out of control because of the state's failure to effect administrative and infrastructural penetration of these remote areas which could not provide a viable surplus in terms of agricultural revenue.

The Taliban is an active component of the overall International Islamic Front (IIF) and the Al Qaeda and thus draws support from the large resources both in terms of funds and manpower from this terrorist conglomerate of sorts. The spread of the Taliban extends in Afghanistan to the South and the East and in Pakistan through the amorphous Tehreek-e-Taliban Pakistan to Waziristan and North West Frontier Province. The Group with its affiliates is able to reach in other areas in Afghanistan in the North and the West as well as to Pakistan's majority Punjab province.

The number of Taliban fighters has been debated. Some say that this is as large as 10,000 while others quote a much smaller figure of 3000. However at any given time a number of local tribal leaders are influenced by the Taliban to support their cause and take on the foreign and Afghan forces supporting them, which indicates that the larger number may be the right one.

The Taliban is not a monolith and there are many other anti government forces. The UN refers to these as AGEs or Anti Government Elements. There are two other prominent groups operating in Afghanistan. In the North is the Hezb-e-Islami under Gulbuddin Hekmatyar, which is active in the Kunar province while the Haqqani network led by Jalauddin Haqqani and his son Sirajuddin Haqqani is active in the Eastern region of Paktia and Paktika extending its influence to Kabul. These two groups apart from the Al Qaeda, form a part of the so called, "strategic assets" of the Pakistani Inter Services Intelligence or ISI. It is the suicide bombers of the Haqqani network who are suspected to have struck at the Indian Embassy in Kabul in July 2008 and again in Oct 2009.. A map showing area of influence of these groups prepared by the Institute for the Study of War is included for reference.

The Taliban command or Shura based in Quetta which some say has split in four groups to avoid being targeted by US drones, and is now located in Peshawar, Karachi and Miranshah controls the overall militancy with individual groups carrying out strikes based on the directive control principle, (though all attacks are generally claimed by the Taliban). Taliban leaders including Mullah Muhammad Omar are based in safe sanctuaries suspected to bc provided by the ISI. Mullah Abdul Ghani Baradar is reported to be the operational commander of the group in Afghanistan. Qari Yousef Ahmadi is another important commander who is also the spokesman of the group. Their main function is to channel the funds, find new recruits and control the overall flow of militancy. There is thus very loose control of the Taliban Shura per se on the local commanders operating in various regions and districts of the country. This provides some scope for local deals and alliances which have been successful in the past to wean away some guerrilla groups. However on the whole there is firm control over the key leaders who are committed to the ideology of the group.

In Pakistan the TTP with leaders as Baitullah Mehsud (who has since been killed in a drone attack), Hafiz Gul Bahadur and Maulavi Nazir, the latter again supported by the ISI are seen to support the Afghan Taliban providing fighters, training bases and funding where required. Their bases in North and South Waziristan are devoid of government controls (unlike in Afghanistan where the international Security Assistance Force is actively chasing the militants). In February 2009, the TTP and the Afghanistan Taliban arc reported to have formed a united council, or Shura, called the Council of United Mujahedeen.

These groups claim support of the people. Haqqani group leader, Sirajuddin Haqqani, who has major presence in Paktika, Paktia and Khost provinces as well as the capital, Kabul claimed that Afghan intelligence agents routinely share information with militants about U.S. and NATO troop movements. "The people of Afghanistan are with us," said Sirajuddin Haqqani, in an exclusive interview to NBC News. "The Afghan intelligence officials are sympathetic to the Taliban and they communicate the movements of the occupying forces [U.S. and NATO] to us." Haqqani also said that, contrary to comments from U.S. officials, there are no moderate Taliban willing to talk to America. United States recently announced a reward of $5 million on his head.

It is noteworthy that before the elections the Haqqani Shura launched a series of high profile attacks on Kabul, including one on the Presidential Palace itself. Pakistan's COAS was intercepted calling

Haqqani a Strategic Asset after he targeted the Indian Embassy in Kabul in 2008.

The same group has again attacked the Indian Embassy in Kabul on 8 October 2009.This clearly highlights its strong nexus with the ISI.

An important issue highlighted by Sirajuddin Haqqani is the level of support of the locals to the Taliban. While some of it would be coercive, gained through the use of the gun, this has to be negated if success in counter militancy operations is to be achieved. Moreover linkages between the local police and the Taliban appear to be growing for that is evident with a lesser number of bomb and suicide attacks on police and the Afghan Army in the recent past. Therefore these also need to be explored and negated.

The Taliban as an ethnic and cultural force in Afghanistan, will continue to draw its strength from the support that the Pashtuns in the South and East give it. The overall orientation is more anti American rather than extremist Islamism thereby ensuring that the support base is wider (as extremist Islam has limited number of followers in Afghanistan). This ideological mix has enabled it to dilute the hatred generated against it during their rule in the country where women were persecuted and all freedoms curtailed. While the Taliban are still predominantly a Pashtun movement, their appeal among Non-Pashtuns is increasing. *This is due to the deepening sense of occupation, an undercurrent of Anti-Westernism and primarily, writes Thomas Ruttig, the growing anger about the behaviour of the foreign forces.*

The other factor supporting the Taliban is corruption in government and instability. The Taliban emphasise their, "clean" rule devoid of corruption and infighting amongst the warlords to influence the population apart from their anti foreign troops propaganda.

The Afghan government's approach towards the Taliban is seen to be more conciliatory, they are referred to as, "enemies of the state" rather than directly as the Taliban. The government is also aware of the factionalized nature of the groups and thus is successfully targeting them to advantage from time to time, splitting the local Taliban leadership in a number of provinces by offering them the lure of important posts as governor of provinces and other trappings of power. This includes for instance, the Taliban governor of Bamiyan Province, who was in office when the Bamiyan Buddhas were destroyed.

OVERVIEW OF TALIBAN OPERATIONS IN 2009

Post US review of policy and a joint Af-Pak strategy, the Taliban also undertook a parallel appraisal of its policy and organisation of militancy. Mullah Mohammed Omar, gave a call to the Pakistani militant groups to join the battle to "liberate Afghanistan from the occupation forces." The key Pakistan Taliban groups led by Baitullah Mehsud (now killed), Mullah Nazir and Gul Bahadur formed the Shura Ittihad-ul-Mujahideen as brought out earlier. They are sending their fighters into Afghanistan to combat the surge of the US and NATO forces. Thus the areas astride the Durand Line, Southern and Eastern Afghanistan saw increased militant activity.

There is also a significant shift in tactics of the Taliban from frontal attacks or ambushes to include insurgent or guerrilla type activities, including asymmetric attacks such as IEDs, VBIEDs, BBIEDs, (that remain responsible for the largest number of civilian deaths), and targeted assassinations.

While there were reports that the Taliban was getting closer to Kabul they had so far succeeded in planting a number of IEDs and conducting suicide attacks including in the high security zone. On 11 February there was a multiple suicide terrorist attack indicating that penetration was much deeper than had been thought of earlier. Taliban militants killed 28 people in a coordinated attack on three government buildings in Kabul. The attack was launched in three prongs in the high security zone, at about 10 a.m. and was carried out by eight insurgents carrying Kalashnikov rifles, grenades and explosive vests. While all eight attackers died, they reportedly communicated with a militant leader in Pakistan. "As they were entering the Ministry of Justice and before starting the indiscriminate killing of the civilians there, they sent three messages to Pakistan, calling for the blessing of their mastermind," Afghan Foreign Ministry spokesperson Saleh told a news conference.

There have also been a number of similar multiple attacks on other government facilities. Thus as per UNAMA Report on 1 April 2009, there was a multiple attack on the Provincial Council building in Kandahar City. This was started by a car bomb at the compound's gate to facilitate the entry of six armed men bearing AK-47s and wearing suicide vests. Two of the attackers were killed in the car bomb but the other four entered the building, two of whom detonated the vest while two were shot and killed. The total deaths suffered by the government and civilians were three government officials, four Provincial Council employees, and seven ANP guards, 17 civilians were injured.[14]

Another complex attack was the one on the Provincial Council and the Governor's compound in Kandahar in April. There is also a concern therefore of the deterioration in the security situation in Kandahar with the American focus shifting to neighbouring Helmand, it is said that Kandahar has seen a rise in incidents to the tune of 80 per cent compared with 2008 particularly in terms of incidents involving improvised explosive devices reported in the city.[15]

In a similar attack launched on the Provincial Administration in Khost on 12 May 2009, 21 individuals were killed, including three civilians, and 25 individuals were injured. At about 11:00, a group of AGE simultaneously attacked the office of the Provincial Governor and the ANP HQ using explosives, heavy weapons and small arms fire. The attack on the Governor's Office was carried out by a VBIED and then a BBIED attacker was wearing a burqa. They occupied the government buildings and carried out heavy firing till the area was cordoned off and cleared by the ISAF and ANA forces. Khost was specifically targeted because of the large presence of international military forces.

Thus it would be seen that the intensity and spread of Taliban operations has greatly increased in 2009. So far, the impact of the US surge has been limited though it may show better results in the second half of the year and thus a firm conclusion cannot be drawn. Nevertheless there is an increase in the overall level of Taliban violence in 2009 so far.

Pakistani Support. Serving and retired personnel of the ISI and the Frontier Corps have been providing significant levels of support to the Taliban. This includes logistics support, medical treatment of the wounded Talibs, sharing of intelligence about the ANA, US and NATO forces and above all training support. Training is being imparted to the Taliban and other terrorist groups at Quetta, Manshera, Shamshattu and Parchinar. To avoid detection by the Americans, a number of retired officers and men of the ISI (of the Afghan Jihad vintage) have been recalled /reemployed to interact with the Taliban.

CIVILIAN CASUALTIES

Civilian casualties in Afghanistan are a major cause for denuding support to the international presence and operations in the country. This is frequently manipulated by the Taliban to advantage. In the first six months of 2009, UNAMA recorded 1013 civilian deaths, compared with 818 for the same period in 2008, and 684 in 2007. This is an increase by 24% of civilian casualties in the first six months of 2009 as compared to the same period in 2008. These casualties are attributable to the Taliban and to pro-government forces (PGF). However more civilians are being killed by AGEs than by PGF. In the first six months of 2009, 59% of civilians were killed by AGEs and 30.5% by PGF. This represents a significant shift from 2007 when PGF were responsible for 41% and AGEs for 46% of civilian deaths.[17]

On the civilian deaths between January and June 2009, 595 were attributed to AGE activities; 400 of those deaths were the result of indiscriminate IED and suicide attacks. This represents 67% of all deaths attributable to AGEs, or 39.5% of the total 1013 civilians killed in the first half of 2009.[18] The details have been covered as per graphs below.

The Taliban frequently undertake operations regardless of the impact on civilians in terms of deaths and injuries or destruction of civilian infrastructure. The Taliban or AGEs are also basing themselves in civilian areas to blur the distinction between combatants and civilians, and to draw in a military response by the government forces thus leading to civilian casualties.[19] IED attacks are also being carried out on roads used by civilian traffic, residential compounds, and market places and also include targeted assassinations of civilians through the use of IEDs, particularly in the South-East.[20]

#1 Recorded civilian casualties January-June 2007-2009*

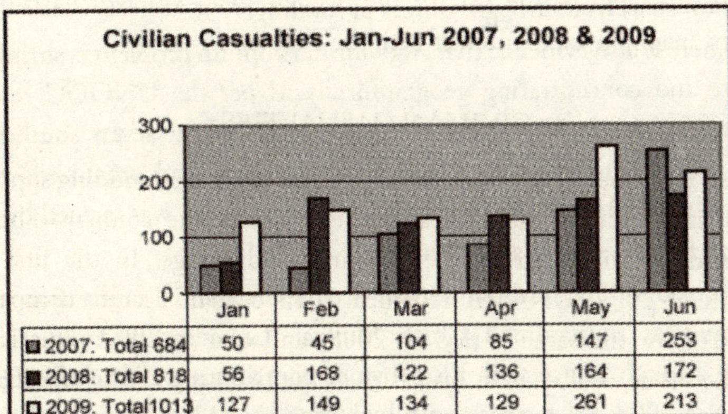

[*Source:* UNAMA[21]]

THE DRUG AND FINANCIAL NETWORK SUPPORTING THE TALIBAN

The United Nations Office of Drugs and Crime (UNODC) survey on drug economy of Afghanistan which sustains the Taliban financially in a major way apart from crime and other forms of malign financial activities has indicated a decline in the source of revenues year on year.[22] In 2007 the (farm gate) value of opium cultivation was about $1 billion. In 2008 it dropped by more than a quarter to $730 million. In 2007 the (potential) export value of opium, morphine and heroin (at border prices in neighbouring countries) was $4 billion. The 2008 drug export was valued at $3.4 billion. In many parts of Afghanistan, authorities impose a charge (called ushr) on economic activity, traditionally set at 10% of income. Thus, opium farming may have generated $50-$70 million of such tax income in 2008.

Furthermore, opium processing and trafficking may have raised an additional $200-$400 million. Thus rebel tribal leaders, drug-lords and insurgents will have extracted almost half a billion dollars of tax revenue from drug farming, production and trafficking as per UNODC estimates published in November 2008. This is the most resilient source of income for the Taliban which has thus sustained its capacity to wage a large scale rebellion apart from foreign sources of funding.[23]

There is also evidence that Afghanistan's opium problem is shrinking in size and concentrating geographically as per the UNODC report. Afghan opium is now grown exclusively (98%) in seven south-west provinces, where insurgents control the territory and organized crime groups benefit from their protection. In 2008 opium was farmed by one million fewer people than in 2007.[24]

The UNODC estimates that decline in opium cultivation may continue, as Mohammad Gulab Mangal, Governor of Helmand, is taking a tough stance with his province contributing 2/3 of all Afghan opium in 2008. Price trends with high food prices is motivating farmers to stick to food crops. These and other incentives as subsidies may wean away the Afghan farmer from poppy cultivation, a major source of income for the Taliban. A graph showing the same is enclosed for reference.

Opium Cultivation in Afghanistan (ha), 1994-2008

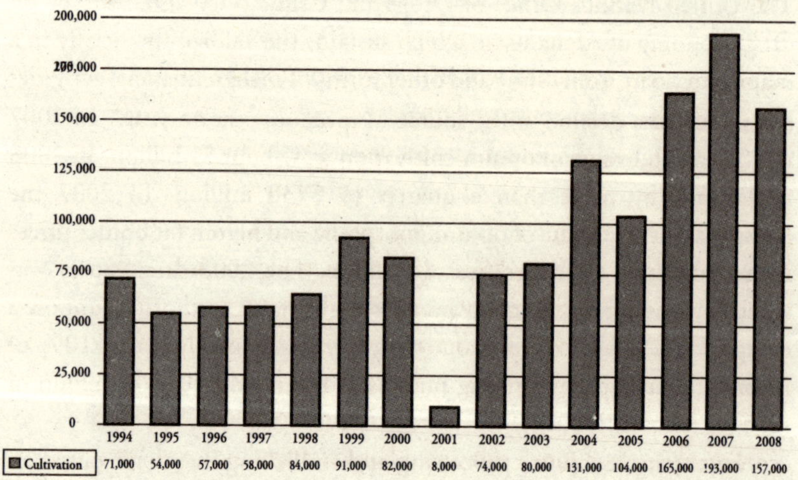

[*Source:* UNODC Afghan Opium Survey 2008[25].]

CONCLUSION

The rise in levels of militancy as gauged from the number of incidents and increasing shift of the Taliban tactics to cause heavy casualties to the ISAF and the Afghan National Army such as use of roadside IEDs and upscaling level of attacks to complex terrorist strikes is a major cause of concern in 2009. Gen. Stanley McChrystal the US commander in Afghanistan warned that U.S. casualties, which have greatly increased in July 2009 are likely to remain high in the months ahead given that the strategy has shifted to that of security and safety of the people.[26]

Gen. McChrystal's assessment of the militancy indicates a geographical spread from the traditional south and east to stable areas in the north and west.[27] Thus from Uruzgan, Helmand, Kandahar, and Zabol Provinces in the South and Paktia, Paktika, Kunar, Ghazni in the East it is said to extend to other areas in the West and North. However an analysis of incidents does not reveal that the situation in these areas is alarming as the attacks remain sporadic.

The American strategy is to extend the security grid by deploying additional troops which is still in its early stages and under constant pressure. The casualties are mounting due to IEDs given that there are now a greater number of active targets which can be engaged by the Taliban.[28] Establishing security grids is a classic counter insurgency approach and if sustained will enable overcoming the hold of the Taliban in many areas in the South and the east.

The Afghan President is seeking a fresh approach to negotiate agreements with the ISAF for more control over foreign troops in the country.[29] The question of talks with moderate Taliban is another option but would have to first address who these moderate Taliban are, what is their loyalty and will they stick to the promises they make and for how long? There is support in Afghanistan for talks with the Taliban and therefore this factor may play an increasingly important role in the days ahead. However the core Taliban around Mullah Omar would not compromise, therefore a soft and a hard strategy to bring down the level of violence by physically reducing the number of militants in the mainstream would have to be adopted.[30]

Thus amidst rising gloom there is also hope as the support to the Taliban from various sources including drugs and crime is likely to go down, the reach of governance will increase with establishment of the security grid, drone operations in Pakistan may take out more Taliban and Al Qaeda leaders as Baitullah Mehsud and Islamabad will sustain the pressure on the Taliban in its areas with a corresponding effort by ISAF in Afghanistan. When combined with enhanced capacity of the Afghan National Army and police, the Taliban and the Al Qaeda could be placed under increased pressure in the year ahead. However with time on their side, the Taliban would attempt to wait for signs of breakup of international resolve in Afghanistan and that would be their core objective in the near future.

Capacity Building of the ANA. The Key to victory in Afghanistan lies in a rapid capacity building of the ANA. The proposed size of 134,000 straight legged infantry force, is far too unrealistic. At the very least there is an urgent case to raise it to the level of the Afghan Army left behind by the Soviets in 1989 (550,000 strong). The Americans have spent over $250 billion in Afghanistan so far. The bulk of it has been spent on sustaining their small military contingent and its cost of operations. It would have been far more cost-effective to rapidly expand the size and capacity of the Afghan Army and let it do the bulk of the heavy lifting. This was the core of the largely successful Soviet counter Guerilla Policy. It is of paramount importance that the conflict be nativised at the earliest. The cost of expanding the ANA to triple its current grossly inadequate size, would, in real cost-benefit terms, be far less than the comparative cost of sustaining US/NATO troops. Besides it would greatly dilute local hostility. This alone can provide security to the population and enable the actualization of the Clear, Hold, Build strategy. Nativizing the conflict is the key to victory. It is here that India can help by rapidly raising and equipping upto Two ANA Divisions.

Border Fencing—Key to Ammunition Management: As per Indian military experience in CI operations, a key component of the defeat mechanism is curtailing the ammunition supply of the insurgents and their free movement to and from their sanctuaries. This can be achieved by physical barriers like fencing. This solution had worked very well in

Punjab and later in J&K. The disruption of the LTTEs ammunition supply was a key component of its defeat mechanism. It would assist greatly if the Americans could prevail upon Pakistan to fence the border with Afghanistan. It could in fact prove to be a battle winning factor.

Replicating the Soviet Strategy: It is important to closely study the Soviet strategy simply because it had been largely successful. The Soviets focused upon holding the cities and key lines of communication and rapidly rebuilding the Afghan Army and Secret Police. They mentored it for four to five years in actual operations, and when they were confident of its combat capabilities; increasingly shifted the bulk of ground combat to the local forces and then withdrew. This is precisely what the Americans need to do. They will have to strengthen the surge to put the Taliban under severe military pressure. Without this there is simply no way that it can be compelled to negotiate. These negotiations themselves will serve to curtail its activity levels and create the conditions for a rapid expansion of the Afghan Army. A rapid capacity building of the ANA alone will lead to victory and a stabilsation of the Afghan state.

The Role of Airpower: In the absence of adequate boots on the ground there is simply no way that the US/NATO forces can reduce their reliance upon airpower. This serves to increase collateral damage and further alienates the population. However if the Americans are not willing or capable of such troop accretions, they will have to continue to rely upon air-power despite its constraints. For the sake of national prestige and long term security, the Americans will have to stay engaged in Afghanistan. Any premature attempts to thin out ground troops prescence and rely unduly upon Predator operations could lead to a long term security disaster.

APPENENDIX

Broad Time Line in Afghanistan

Oct. 7, 2001: U.S. and British planes begin bombing to root out al Qaeda leader Osama bin Laden and his Taliban protectors.

Nov. 13: Anti-Taliban Northern Alliance forces enter Kabul.

Dec. 5: Afghan groups sign deal in Bonn on interim government headed by ethnic Pashtun tribal leader Hamid Karzai.

June 19, 2002: Karzai sworn in as president for 18 months.

Oct. 9, 2004: Presidential election. Karzai declared winner and sworn in on Dec. 7.

Sept. 18, 2005: Elections for a lower house of parliament and provincial councils. Parliament sits for first time on Dec. 19.

Jan. 31, 2006: Afghanistan receives pledges of $10.5 billion to help it fight poverty and the drug trade and improve security.

July 30: NATO forces take control of security in the south, moving from Kabul and the safer north and west.

Oct. 5: NATO's International Security Assistance Force (ISAF) assumes responsibility for security in all of Afghanistan.

March 2, 2007: Pakistani security forces capture Mullah Obaidullah Akhund, the Taliban's third most senior leader, in Quetta.

May 13: Mullah Dadullah, a Taliban commander in the south, killed in a clash with Western and Afghan forces in Helmand.

June 12, 2008: Donors pledge about $20 billion in aid at a Paris conference, but say Kabul must do far more to fight corruption.

July 7: Suicide car bomb hits Indian embassy in Kabul, killing 41 people.

Aug. 19: Suspected Taliban insurgents kill 10 French troops and wound 21 in ambush east of the capital, the biggest single loss of foreign forces in combat in Afghanistan since 2001.

Dec. 5: Karzai and new Pakistani President Asif Ali Zardari pledge to boost cooperation and agree a joint strategy to fight al Qaeda and other militants along their shared border.

Jan. 27, 2009: Thousands of U.S. troops move into two key

provinces in east Afghanistan as part of strategy of outgoing U.S. President George W. Bush's administration. [ID:nISL340081]

Feb. 17: New U.S. President Barack Obama orders 17,000 more U.S. troops to tackle an intensifying insurgency. [ID:nN17387736]

March 27: Obama announces plans to send a further 4,000 U.S. troops to train Afghan Security Forces, along with civilian personnel to improve delivery of basic services. [ID:nN26525038]

March 29: Karzai announces he will stay in office after his term officially ends on May 21 until elections are held in August. He later says he'll run for re-election. [ID:nLT70652]

May 11: Top U.S. and NATO commander in Afghanistan General David McKiernan is fired by Obama. His exit signals a shift from a conventional strategy to a counter-insurgency plan, aimed at lessening civilian deaths. [ID:nN11540962]

June 15: U.S. General Stanley McChrystal assumes command of international troops in Afghanistan. [ID:nISL126144]

July 2: U.S. Marines launch assault in lower Helmand river valley in southern Afghanistan.

July 27: Britain announces the end of a five-week Operation "Panther's Claw," the largest offensive by British forces since mid-2006, saying it had succeeded in driving militants out of population centres ahead of elections.

Aug. 15: Taliban claims responsibility for a suicide car bomb that killed seven people and wounded 100 outside the NATO-led ISAF Headquarters in Kabul, near the US Embassy.

REFERENCES

1. Based on analysis of incidents by the author from January to July 2009.
2. UNAMA Report. AFGHANISTAN Mid Year Bulletin on Protection of Civilians in Armed Conflict, 2009. July 2009. [Kabul: UNAMA]. p. 5.
3. Based on analysis of incidents by the author from January to July 2009.
4. UNAMA Report. AFGHANISTAN Mid Year Bulletin on Protection of Civilians in Armed Conflict, 2009. July 2009. [Kabul: UNAMA]. p. 9.
5. General Assembly Security Council. The situation in Afghanistan and its implications for international peace and security Report of the Secretary-General 23 June 2009. [New York: UN] p. 5.

6. UNAMA Report. AFGHANISTAN Mid Year Bulletin on Protection of Civilians in Armed Conflict, 2009. July 2009. [Kabul: UNAMA]. p. 10.
7. UNAMA Report. AFGHANISTAN Mid Year Bulletin on Protection of Civilians in Armed Conflict, 2009. July 2009. [Kabul: UNAMA]. P. UNAMA Report. AFGHANISTAN Mid Year Bulletin on Protection of Civilians in Armed Conflict, 2009. July 2009. [Kabul: UNAMA]. p. 5.
8. UNAMA Report. AFGHANISTAN Mid Year Bulletin on Protection of Civilians in Armed Conflict, 2009. July 2009. [Kabul: UNAMA]. p. 5.
9. UNAMA Report. AFGHANISTAN Mid Year Bulletin on Protection of Civilians in Armed Conflict, 2009. July 2009. [Kabul: UNAMA]. p. 5.
10. UNAMA Report. AFGHANISTAN Mid Year Bulletin on Protection of Civilians in Armed Conflict, 2009. July 2009. [Kabul: UNAMA]
11. UNAMA Report. AFGHANISTAN Mid Year Bulletin on Protection of Civilians in Armed Conflict, 2009. July 2009. [Kabul:
12. UNAMA UNODC. Afghan Opium Survey 2008. [Geneva: UNODC].
13. UNODC. Afghan Opium Survey 2008. [Geneva: UNODC].
14. UNODC. Afghan Opium Survey 2008. [Geneva: UNODC].
15. UNODC. Afghan Opium Survey 2008. [Geneva: UNODC].
16. Yochi J Dreazen. Peter Spiegel. Taliban Now Winning. Available at http://online.wsj.com/article/SB124986154654218153.html
17. Yochi J Dreazen. Peter Spiegel. Taliban Now Winning. Available at http://online.wsj.com/article/SB124986154654218153.html
18. Yochi J Dreazen. Peter Spiegel. Taliban Now Winning. Available at http://online.wsj.com/article/SB124986154654218153.html
19. Yochi J Dreazen. Peter Spiegel. Taliban Now Winning. Available at http://online.wsj.com/article/SB124986154654218153.html
20. Based on analysis of incidents by the author from January to July 2009.
21. Taliban Time Line. Reuters Brief. Available at http://www.reuters.com/article/latestCrisis/idUSSP519740. Accessed on 16 August 2009.

•

4

Analysis of Key Drivers: Demographic, Economic and Geo-Political

DEMOGRAPHICS

An analysis of the demographic factors is critical to the understanding of the insurgency in Afghanistan, and in fact holds the key to state formation and collapse in that country. This chapter will therefore take a detailed look at the key drivers of demography, ethnic groupings, economy and the geopolitical factors that will shape the flow of events in Afghanistan.

STATISTICS

According to the CIA World Fact book, Afghanistan's demographic profile is as follows:

Population:	33,609,937 (July 2009 est.)	
Age structure:	0-14 years	– 44.5%
	15-64 years	– 53%
	65 years and over	– 2.4% (2009 est.)
Median age:	Total: 17.6 years	
	Male: 17.6 years	
	Female: 17.6 years (2009 est.)	

Population Growth

Rate:	2.629% (2009 est.)
Birth rate:	45.46 births / 1,000 population (2009 est.)
Death rate:	19.56 deaths / 1,000 population (2008 est.)
Net migration rate:	21 migrant(s)/1,000 population (2009 est.)

Sex ratio: At birth: 1.05 malc(s)/female
Under 15 years: 1.05 male(s)/female
15-64 years: 1.05 male(s)/female
65 years and over: 0.93 male(s)/female
Total population: 1.05 male(s)/female (2009 est.)

Infant mortality rate: Total: 151.95 deaths/1,000 live births
Male: 156.01 deaths/1,000 live births
Female: 147.7 deaths/1,000 live births (2009 est.)

Life expectancy at birth: Total population: 44.64 years
Male: 44.47 years
Female: 44.81 years (2009 est.)

Total fertility rate: 6.53 children born/woman (2009 est.)

HIV/AIDS - Adult Prévalence Rate: 0.01% (2001 est.)

Total expenditure on health as % of GDP (2006): 5.4

Human Development Index Rank

Out of 171 countries: 169

- 57 percent of Afghanistan's population is below 18 years of age. The average household size is seven, with children under 18 accounting for 4 out of 7 people in the household. The population of Afghanistan is increasing rapidly as the total fertility rate is estimated to be 6.3 per woman. The population of men outgrows that of women. The overall population growth rate over the past three decades of conflict is estimated at 2.5 percent per year. The limited access to health facilities implies that many women are repeatedly exposed to the risk of disease, disability and health during pregnancy, labor, birth and post natal recovery. Maternal mortality in Afghanistan is assumed to be one of the highest in the world. The maternal mortality ratio is 1,600 per 100,000 live births. Indicating that the male member might be dead or displaced, a female heads 3.3 percent of households. Under five mortality is estimated at 172 and infant mortality at 115 per 1000 live births—one of the highest in the world. Afghanistan is ranked fourth by having the highest under five-mortality rate in the world.

- Afghanistan remains one of the countries with the poorest health indicators. It is lacking some major and important health indicators especially in the field of reproductive health and health care financing. The government with credible assistance from the international community is involved in imparting education and health services to people besides improving road, telecommunication and electricity to provide minimum required essential facilities in the war-ravaged country.

GEO-POLITICAL DRIVERS

Ethnicity is the key complexity in Afghanistan. An understanding of this aspect is vital for its overriding impact on state formation and politics in that country. The ethnic breakdown is a highly sensitive and contested issue. The key aspect is that though the Pashtuns are the largest ethnic group, they do not constitute a majority. Besides, the Pashtuns are deeply divided on tribal faultlines. Post the Taliban however, ethnicity has become a major faultline between the Pashtuns and the Farsiwans. In fact so explosive is the issue that a national census was postponed till 2010.

Afghanistan's ethnic groups primarily consist of the following:

Ethnic Groupings:

Pashtun	36.4% - 42%
Tajik	27% - 38.1%
Hazara	8.0% - 9.2%
Uzbek	8.0% - 9.2%
Aimak	0.1% - 4%
Turkmen	1.7% - 3%
Baloch	0.5% - 4%
Others	1.9% - 9.2%

(Pashai, Hindki, Nuristani, Brahui and Hindkowans)

Pashtun: Also known as Pakhtun or Pathan, or ethnic Afghans who reside mainly in southern and eastern Afghanistan and also in western Pakistan. Considerable pockets exist throughout other parts of

Afghanistan as Pashtuns have migrated in the recent past or have been forcefully displaced, to northern and western regions. Smaller groups of Pashtuns are also found in Iran. It is believed that the Pashtuns emerged from the area around the Sulaiman Mountains (western frontier mountains of India) and expanded from there onwards. The Afghan identity began to develop as a 'Pashtun' identity under the rule of Ahmad Shah Durrani who united the Pashtun (Afghan) chiefdoms in the middle of 18th century. The strong and visible ethnic divide all across the country continues with Pashtuns dominating in all spheres of national activity.

Tajik: The Persian-speaking Tajiks are closely related to the Persians of Iran. Sub-groups of the Tajiks include the Farsiwan and the Qizilbash. The major difference between them is that they are generally of the Shia sect while other Tajiks are of the Sunni sect. In modern day Afghanistan, Tajiks have been known mainly for being bureaucrats, educationists, doctors, teachers, professors, cultural artisans and successful merchants and entrepreneurs.

Hazara: The Hazaras constitute a Persian-speaking group residing mainly in the Hazarajat region. The Hazaras are known to have partial Mongolian origins with some admixture from surrounding indigenous groups. Linguistically the Hazaras speak a dialect of Persian, known as Hazaragi and sometimes their variant is interspersed with more Mongolian words. There is a common belief among many Afghans that the Hazaras are descendants of Genghis Khan's army, which marched into the area during the 12th century. Unlike most Afghans, the Hazaras belong to the Shia sect, which has often set them apart from their neighbors. There is a sizeable Hazara community in Pakistan particularly in NWFP and Quetta as well as in Iran.

Uzbek: The Uzbeks mainly are Turkic people of Afghanistan and are found mainly in the northern regions of the country. The Uzbeks in all likelihood migrated with a wave of Turkic invaders and intermingled with local Iranian tribes over time to become the ethnic group they are today. Uzbeks mostly are Sunni Muslims and are closely related to the Turkmen found in Afghanistan. The Uzbeks of Afghanistan are usually bilingual, fluent in both Persian and Uzbek. Physically, the Uzbek are generally Mongoloid in appearance.

Turkmen: The Turkmen are the smaller Turkic group who can also be found in neighboring Turkmenistan and [Iran] particularly around Mashad. Largely Sunni Muslims, their origins are very similar to that of the Uzbeks. Unlike, the Uzbeks, however, the Turkmen are traditionally a nomadic people (though they were forced to abandon this way of life in Turkmenistan itself under Soviet rule).

Baloch: The Baloch are another Iranian ethnic group that numbers around 200,000 in Afghanistan. The main Baloch areas are located in Balochistan province in Pakistan and Sistan and Balochistan province of Iran. Many also live in southern Afghanistan. They are offshoots of the Kurds, mainly pastoral and desert dwellers and are Sunni Muslim.

Nuristani: The Nuristani are an Indo-Iranian tribe, representing a fourth independent branch of the Aryan race (Indo-Aryan, Iranian, Nuristani, and Dardic), who live in isolated regions of northeastern Afghanistan as well as across the border in the district of Chitral in Pakistan. Better known historically as the *Kafirs* from what was once known as Kafiristan (land of pagans), they converted to Islam during the rule of Amir Abdur Rahman and their country was renamed "Nuristan", meaning "Land of Light" (as in the light of Islam). They primarily are Sunni Muslims. Other smaller groups include *Wakhis, Pashai, Aimak, Kyrgyz, Brahui,* and *Arabs.*

Linguistic Groups: In the *Constitutional Loya Jirga* (CLJ), language also became a major bone of contention. The Pashtuns wanted the Pashto language to be the national language, whereas the Farsiwans were in favour of Dari (Afghan Persian). Dari has now been adopted as the official language along with Pashto. Percentage breakdown of languages spoken are:

Afghan Persian or Dari (official)	50%
Pashto (official)	35%
Turkic languages (primarily Uzbek and Turkmen)	11%
30 minor languages (primarily Balochi and Pashai)	4%

The demographics of Afghanistan are ethnically and linguistically mixed. This reflects its location astride historic trade and invasion routes leading from Central Asia into South Asia and Southwest Asia.

Afghanistan can be considered a country of cluster of minorities, as there is no group serving as a majority. Pashtuns remain the largest ethnic group followed by the Tajiks as the second largest group, then Hazaras, Uzbeks tied for third, followed by the Aimak, Turkmen, Baluch, Nuristani and other small groups. Pashto and Persian (Dari) are the two official languages of the country. Persian is spoken by nearly half of the population and serves as a lingua franca for most. Pashto is spoken widely in the south, east and southwest. Uzbek and Turkmen are spoken in the north. Smaller groups throughout the country also speak more than 70 other languages and numerous dialects. 2006-07 witnessed the largest refugee return in the world in a generation.

REFUGEES AND INTERNALLY DISPLACED PERSONS (IDPS)

Mostly Pashtuns and Kuchis have been displaced in south and west due to drought and instability. In addition to the displaced, according to the United Nations High Commissioner for Refugees (UNHCR), which played a key part in the process, between January 1, 2002 and December 31, 2007, as many as 4,997,455 refugees returned to Afghanistan. Afghanistan has experienced the largest refugee repatriation in the world in the last 30 years. The return of refugees is guided by the Ministry of Refugees and Repatriation (MORR) and supported by the UNHCR, International Organization of Migration (IOM), United Nations Children's Fund (UNICEF), the World Food Program (WFP), the World Health Organization (WHO), and a number of other national and international NGOs and donors. As of December 2007, approximately 3.5 million Afghans remained in neighboring countries. The US provided more than $447.5 million in support to Afghan refugees, returnees, and other conflict victims between September 2001 and December 2007.

It is striking that even in 2006 and 2007 (years of considerable conflict in parts of Afghanistan) the returns continued, albeit at a reduced rate. In the whole period 2000-2007, the overwhelming majority of refugees have been concentrated in two countries: Iran, from where 1.6 million returned, and Pakistan, from where 3.3 million returned. At the end of 2007 Afghanistan was still the leading country of origin of refugees worldwide, with 3.1 million remaining outside the country. Thus in 2008, even after these returns, Afghan refugees constitute 27% of the entire global refugee population.

Kabul today faces the unrelenting problem of a large number of refugees who have returned from Pakistan. Simultaneously on the other hand, the original inhabitants of Kabul have moved out since the time of the Soviet occupation and the hard-line Taliban regime. However, not all returnees were fully voluntary. Within the countries of asylum there have been heavy pressures on these refugees to return, including the closing of some camps. Many returning refugees have included lack of employment opportunities in Afghanistan, and in some cases involvement in property disputes. There also has been mismanagement and corruption in the Afghan Ministry of Refugees and Repatriation. Refugees live in dire conditions in makeshift settlements. All this has led to considerable disappointment, bitterness and anti-government feelings. As displacement continues, the past two years has seen unknown numbers of returnees having left the country yet again. The number of internally displaced persons within Afghanistan has also increased, especially due to the fighting in the south, and now stands at about 235,000. Some returnees have seamlessly become internally displaced persons.

RELIGIOUS FACTORS

Religions:	*Sunni Muslim*	80%
	Shia Muslim	19%
	Others	1%

99 percent of Afghanistan's population adheres to Islam. An estimated 80 percent of the population is Sunni, following the Hanafi School of jurisprudence. 19 percent is predominantly Shia. Primarily, Islamic practices pervade all aspects of life. Likewise, Islamic religious tradition and codes, together with traditional practices, provide the principal means of controlling personal conduct and settling legal disputes. Excluding urban populations in the principal cities, most

Afghans are divided into tribal and other kinship-based groups, which follow traditional customs and religious practices. The religious element in Afghan politics did not disappear with the departure of Soviet forces in 1989. Indeed, within a few years, religious warriors trained in the hard school of combat against Soviet forces in Afghanistan, turned up in a wide range of other locations, including the former Yugoslavia. These legacies of war against the Soviet control remain most important in Afghanistan. The problems of non-state violence, regional rivalries and the religious element in politics are not new to Afghanistan, but they have been reinforced. Above all, the old instinctive suspicion of foreign projects still remains.

POLITICAL INSTITUTIONS

Government

Type:		Islamic Republic
Independence:		August 19, 1919
Constitution:		January 4, 2004
Branches:	*Executive*—	President (Chief of State).
	Legislative—	Bicameral National Assembly Wolesi Jirga (Lower House)-249 seats Meshrano Jirga (Upper House)-102 seats
	Judicial—	Supreme Court, High Courts and Appeals Courts
Political subdivisions:		34 Provinces.
Suffrage:		Universal at 18 years.

- When Afghanistan held its first national democratic presidential election in October 2004, more than 8 million Afghans voted, 41 percent of which were women. Hamid Karzai was announced as the official winner on November 3 and inaugurated on December 7 for a five-year term as Afghanistan's first democratically elected president. Karzai won 55.4 percent of the vote, in an election that was the nation's first national election since 1969. The National Legislature composed of the House of the People and the House of the Elders was elected on September 18, 2005. This was in addition to the members of the Supreme Court that were appointed by the President to constitute the judiciary. Together, this new system was formed to provide a new set of checks and balances that was unheard of in Afghanistan. While supporters have lauded President Karzai's efforts to promote national reconciliation and a growing economy, critics charge him with failing to stem corruption and the growing drug trade, and the slow pace of reconstruction.

- The current parliament elected in 2005 included former Mujahideen, Taliban members, communists, reformists, and Islamic fundamentalists. Surprisingly, 28 percent of the delegates elected were women, 03 percent more than the 25 percent minimum guaranteed under the constitution. This made Afghanistan, long known under the Taliban for its oppression of women, one of the leading countries in terms of female representation. Chief Justice Abdul Salam Azimi currently leads the Supreme Court of Afghanistan. Dominated by fundamentalist religious figures, it tried to ban a candidate in the 2004 presidential election for questioning polygamy laws, and limited the rights of women, as well as overstepped its constitutional authority by issuing rulings on subjects not yet brought before the court.
- An election was held on September 18, 2005 for the "Wolesi Jirga" (lower house) of Afghanistan's new bicameral National Assembly and for the country's 34 provincial councils. Turnout for the election was about 53 percent of the 12.5 million registered voters. The Afghan constitution provides for indirect election of the National Assembly's "Meshrano Jirga" (upper house) by the provincial councils and by reserved presidential appointments.

The new constitution of Afghanistan has introduced a concept of National Assembly constituting the Wolesi Jirga and Mashrano Jirga along with a modern judicial system. Under the new constitution, the traditional institutions such as Loya Jirga or the meetings of the tribal chiefs and the Shura that were established in order to deliver tribal justice fail to find any place. Critics argue that the old system having traditional institutions caused further fragmentation of the Afghan society due to existing ethnic and tribal loyalties. There has been hope that the new unitary system would help in instilling the concept of nationhood among the Afghan citizens. However, it should be noted that building new institutions from scratch would be a long-drawn process. The transition phase in between could lead to a great deal of ambiguity that ultimately might erode the authority of the central government.

Significantly, the new constitution does not provide for the elected representation at the provincial level. As a result of this, the provincial governors are being appointed primarily on the basis of their loyalty towards President Hamid Karzai. Mostly, they are the same old warlords assuming new roles and power, thereby reinforcing the oppressive regimes of the earlier times. There is considerable disenchantment among the people with the central government in some of the provinces. Afghanistan will undergo a series of elections in 2009-2010. National Assembly elections are scheduled for summer 2010. Elections for district and village councils may also be held in 2010. Unlike previous election cycles, the Afghanistan Independent Election Commission (IEC) will coordinate the elections with assistance from the UN.

Critics state that introduction of an elected federal set up would weaken the government at the centre and further jeopardise the security and development process in the country. There should be concerted efforts to engage sections of the population that is willing to turn away from violence and contribute towards building stable and effective pluralistic and national institutions that would aim towards protecting the interests of all Afghans. Notwithstanding the above, there are visible signs of weakening of the authority of the Karzai government, especially in the southern and eastern part of the country. The re-emergence of the Northern Alliance and the Taliban is testament to this development. The war against Al-Qaeda and related terrorists, now based in Pakistan as well as Afghanistan, is continuing. In addition, there was growing resistance in southern Afghanistan to the central government. The insurgency began relatively slowly, so that its seriousness was not recognised during the initial spell. It was commonly labeled the 'Taliban insurgency' a description that might have concealed the possibility that the sources of support for the insurgency have been more numerous than the label 'Taliban' suggests.

- The insurgent movement has drawn on elements of both Afghan and Pashtun nationalism. It has operated alongside traditional forms of social organisation and systems of justice. The recruiting has been facilitated by the high levels of unemployment in Afghanistan and by the fact that it is able to pay its soldiers good money. The willingness to support poppy cultivation adds to its support in certain provinces while exposing the incoherence of the various NATO countries on this issue. The government's authority is said to be growing, although its ability to deliver necessary social services remains largely dependent on funds from the international donor community. US assistance for Afghanistan's reconstruction from fiscal year 2001 to the present totals over $32 billion. Donors pledged continued assistance for the rebuilding of the country at the June 2008 International Afghanistan Support Conference in Paris. Overall, the international community has made multi-year reconstruction and security assistance pledges to Afghanistan totaling over $42 billion.
- With international community support, including more than 40 countries participating in Operation Enduring Freedom and NATO-led International Security Assistance Force (ISAF), the government's capacity to secure Afghanistan's borders to maintain internal order is increasing. Responsibility for security for all of Afghanistan was transferred to ISAF in October 2006. As of November 2008, approximately 70,000 Afghan National Army (ANA) soldiers and nearly 76,000 police, including border and civil order police had received training. In September 2008, the Joint Coordination and Monitoring Board, made up of key donors and the UN Assistance Mission in Afghanistan (UNAMA), approved the Afghan Government's request to increase the size of the ANA from 86,000 to 134,000 soldiers. Reform of the army and police, to include training, is an extensive and ongoing process, and the US is working with NATO and international partners to further develop Afghanistan's National Security Forces.

- Disarmament, Demobilization, and Reintegration (DDR) has also helped to further establish the authority of the Afghan central government. The DDR programme, after receiving 63,000 military personnel, stopped accepting additional candidates in June 2005. Disarmament and demobilization of all of these candidates were completed at the end of June 2006. A follow-on programme targeting illegal militias, the Disbandment of Illegal Armed Groups (DIAG), began in 2005, under the joint auspices of Japan and the United Nations. The DIAG program is still ongoing.

ECONOMY

The Afghan economy has always been deemed to be a rentier economy where the bulk capital for state formation has invariably come from external sources. This pattern continues to persist and the new Afghan state has so far been given a total of US$82billion by the rest of world for ensuring state formation. For the next 10-20 years the Afghan nation state will continue to need some US$8-10billion a year to remain viable. This will include some US$4billion a year for the ANA and Police alone. This figure may well have to be doubled if a viable Armed Force is to be ensured. A statistical analysis of the GDP and related issues is given below:

GDP (purchasing power parity):	$23.03 billion (2008 est.)
GDP (official exchange rate):	$12.85 billion (2008 est.)
GDP - real growth rate:	7.5% (2008 est.)
GDP - per capita (PPP):	$800 (2008 est.)
GDP - composition by sector:	Agriculture: 31%
	Industry: 26%
	Services: 43%

(Data excludes opium production; 2008 est.)

Unemployment rate:	40% (2008 est.)
Population below poverty line:	53% (2003 est.)
Public debt:	External: $1.23 billion to Russia and Multilateral Development Banks (2007)

Inflation rate (consumer prices):	13% (2007 est.)
Agriculture products:	Opium, wheat, fruits, nuts; wool, mutton, sheepskins, lambskins
Oil - production:	0 bbl/day (2007 est.)
Oil - consumption:	5,036 bbl/day (2006 est.)
Natural gas - production:	20 million cu m (2006 est.)
Natural gas - consumption:	20 million cu m (2006 est.)
Natural gas - proven reserves:	49.55 billion cu m (1 January 2008 est.)

Industries: Small-scale industries taking up production of textiles, soap, furniture, shoes, fertilizer, cement; hand-woven carpets in addition to natural gas, coal, and copper are prevalent. The 1979 Soviet invasion and the ensuing civil war destroyed much of the country's limited infrastructure and disrupted normal patterns of economic activity. Gross domestic product had fallen substantially because of loss of labour and capital along with disruption of trade and transport. Continuing internal strife hampered both domestic efforts at reconstruction as well as international aid efforts. However, Afghanistan's economy has grown at a moderate pace since the 2001 fall of the Taliban, albeit from a low base.

In 2004, Afghanistan's GDP grew 17 percent, and in 2005 the GDP grew at 14 percent. However, the drought in 2006 dropped growth to 5.3 percent. In 2007, growth was expected to be 13 percent. In June 2006, Afghanistan and the International Monetary Fund agreed on a 'poverty reduction' and 'growth facility' programme for 2006-2009 that focused on maintaining macroeconomic stability, boosting growth and reducing poverty. Afghanistan is also rebuilding its banking infrastructure through the Afghanistan National Bank. Several government-owned banks are also in the process of being privatized.

The overall effort seems to lay the foundation for a sound and self-sustaining economy, restore Afghan infrastructure to meet increasing demand and needs of their economy.

AGRICULTURE

The main source of income in the country is agriculture. Being pre-dominantly an agro-based economy, Afghan principle export items are mostly agro and horticulture produces. Export of these products picks up after the month of August every year. The major food crops produced include corn, rice, barley, wheat, vegetables, fruits and nuts. The industry is also based on agriculture and pastoral raw materials. The major industrial crops are cotton, tobacco, madder, castor beans and sugar beets. The Afghan economy continues to be overwhelmingly agricultural, despite the fact that only 12 percent of its total land area is arable and less than 6 percent is currently being cultivated.

Agricultural production is constrained by an almost total dependence on erratic winter snows and spring rains for water. The methods implied for irrigation are primitive. There is relatively little use of machines, chemical fertilizers or pesticides. Overall agricultural production dramatically declined following severe drought as well as sustained fighting, instability in rural areas and deteriorated infrastructure. The easing of the drought and the end of civil war produced the largest wheat harvest in 25 years during 2003. Wheat production was an estimated 58 percent higher than in 2002. However, the country still needs to import an estimated one million tonnes of wheat to meet its requirements. Millions of Afghans, particularly in rural areas, remain dependent on food aid.

OPIUM ECONOMY

For more than two millennia, Afghanistan has been at the crossroads of international terrorist violence and became a major contributor to world narcotics production. The establishment of democracy in Afghanistan and the government's measures against cultivation, trade and abuse of opium could be considered as crucial steps towards resolving the vicious opium trade and arms nexus along with the incessant drug problem.

The opium economy of Afghanistan is an intensely complex phenomenon. It is deeply inter-twined into the political structure, civil society and economy of the country. Spawned after decades of civil and military strife, it has chained a poor rural population including farmers, landless labour, small traders, women and children to the mercy of domestic warlords and international crime syndicates that continue to dominate several areas in the south, north and east of the country.

ROAD LINKAGES : IRAN
IRAN
TURKEY
IRAQ
KUWAIT
SAUDI ARABIA
QATAR
BAHRAIN
UNITED ARAB EMIRATES
OMAN
TURKMENISTAN
AFGHANISTAN
PAKISTAN
PERSIAN GULF
GULF OF OMAN
ĀZARBĀYJĀN-E KHĀVARĪ
ARDEBĪL
GĪLĀN
ZANJĀN
KORDESTĀN
HAMADĀN
KERMĀNSHĀH
LORESTĀN
ĪLĀM
MARKAZĪ
TEHRĀN
MĀZANDARĀN
SEMNĀN
KHORĀSĀN
EŞFAHĀN
YAZD
KERMĀN
FĀRS
BŪSHEHR
HORMOZGĀN
KHŪZESTĀN
SĪSTĀN VA BALŪCHESTĀN
Tehrān
Tabrīz
Ardabīl
Rasht
Sārī
Mashhad
Zanjān
Qazvīn
Sanandaj
Hamadān
Kermānshāh
Īlām
Khorramābād
Arāk
Qom
Kāshān
Semnān
Eşfahān
Yazd
Kermān
Shīrāz
Bandar-e Būshehr
Bandar-e 'Abbās
Zāhedān
Ahvāz
Yāsūj
Shahr-e Kord
Baghdad
Kuwait
Manama
Doha
Abu Dhabi
Ashkabad
Herāt
ISLAMIC REPUBLIC OF
IRAN ایران
National capital
Provincial capital
City, town
Airport
International boundary
Provincial boundary
Main road
Secondary road
0 100 200 300 km

ROAD LINKAGES – CENTRAL ASIA

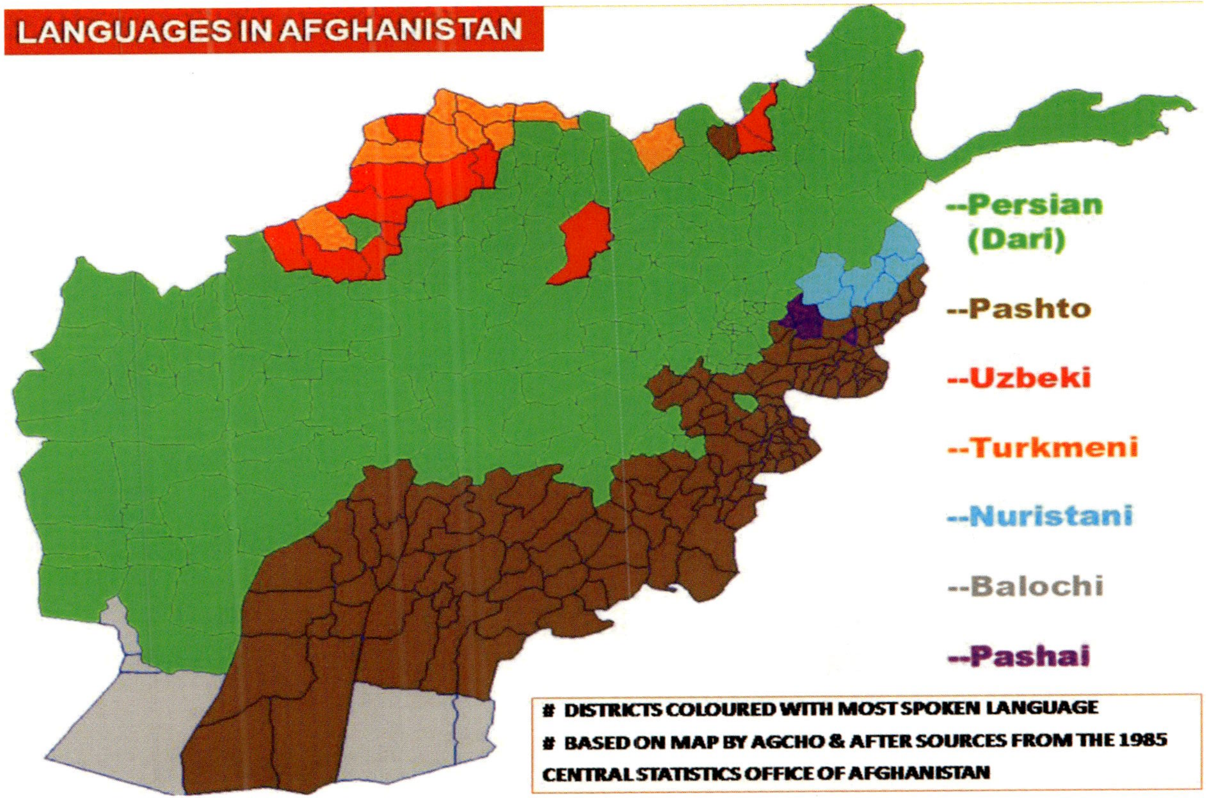
LANGUAGES IN AFGHANISTAN
--Persian (Dari)
--Pashto
--Uzbeki
--Turkmeni
--Nuristani
--Balochi
--Pashai
DISTRICTS COLOURED WITH MOST SPOKEN LANGUAGE
BASED ON MAP BY AGCHO & AFTER SOURCES FROM THE 1985 CENTRAL STATISTICS OFFICE OF AFGHANISTAN

OPIUM POPPY CULTIVATION IN AFGHANISTAN 2007-08

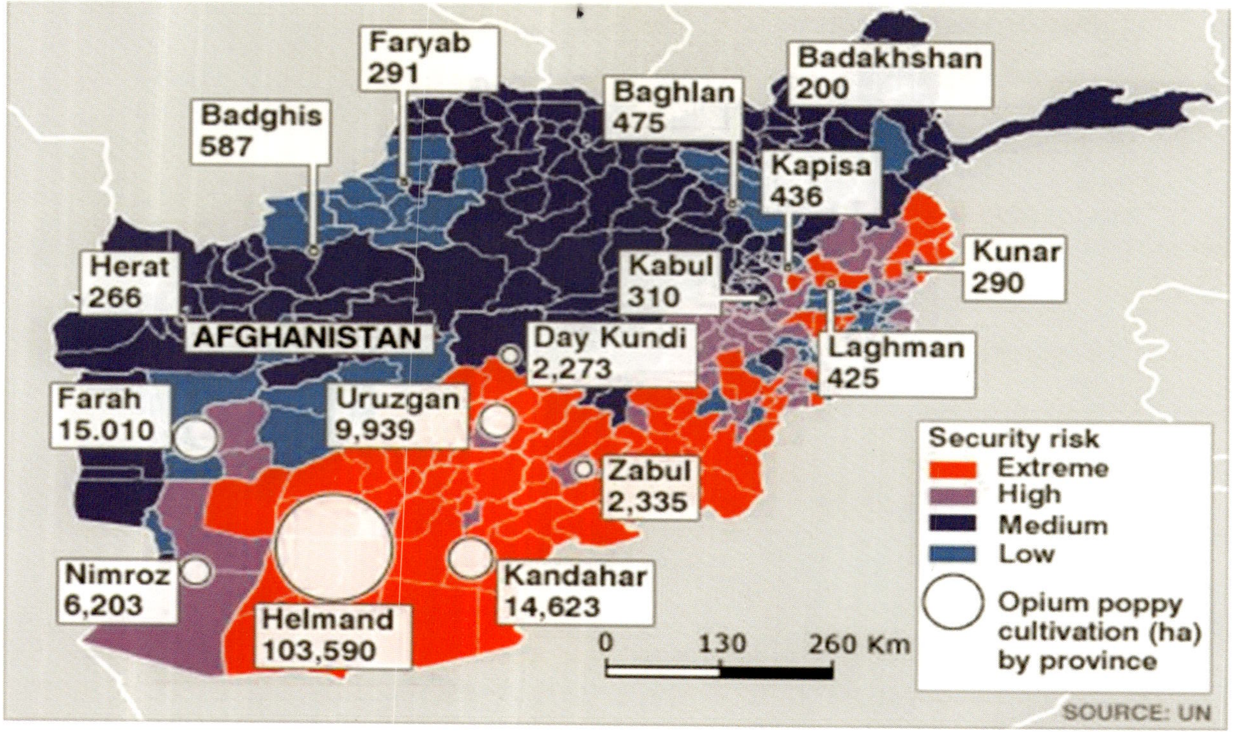

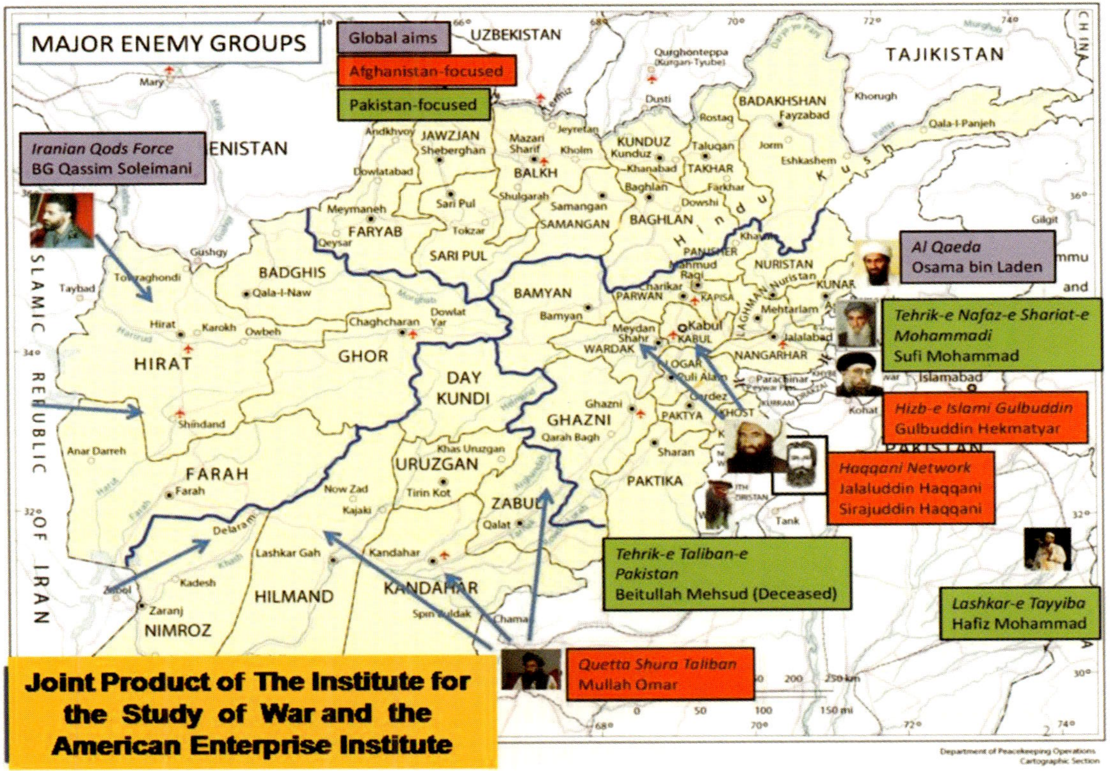
MAJOR ENEMY GROUPS
Global aims
Afghanistan-focused
Pakistan-focused
Iranian Qods Force
BG Qassim Soleimani
Al Qaeda
Osama bin Laden
Tehrik-e Nafaz-e Shariat-e Mohammadi
Sufi Mohammad
Hizb-e Islami Gulbuddin
Gulbuddin Hekmatyar
Haqqani Network
Jalaluddin Haqqani
Sirajuddin Haqqani
Tehrik-e Taliban-e Pakistan
Beitullah Mehsud (Deceased)
Lashkar-e Tayyiba
Hafiz Mohammad
Quetta Shura Taliban
Mullah Omar
Joint Product of The Institute for the Study of War and the American Enterprise Institute
UZBEKISTAN
TAJIKISTAN
CHINA
ISLAMIC REPUBLIC OF IRAN
HIRAT
FARAH
NIMROZ
HILMAND
KANDAHAR
ZABUL
GHAZNI
PAKTIKA
PAKTYA
URUZGAN
DAY KUNDI
GHOR
BADGHIS
FARYAB
JAWZJAN
SARI PUL
BALKH
SAMANGAN
BAGHLAN
KUNDUZ
TAKHAR
BADAKHSHAN
BAMYAN
WARDAK
PARWAN
LOGAR
KABUL
NANGARHAR
NURISTAN
KUNAR
Kabul
Islamabad
Department of Peacekeeping Operations
Cartographic Section

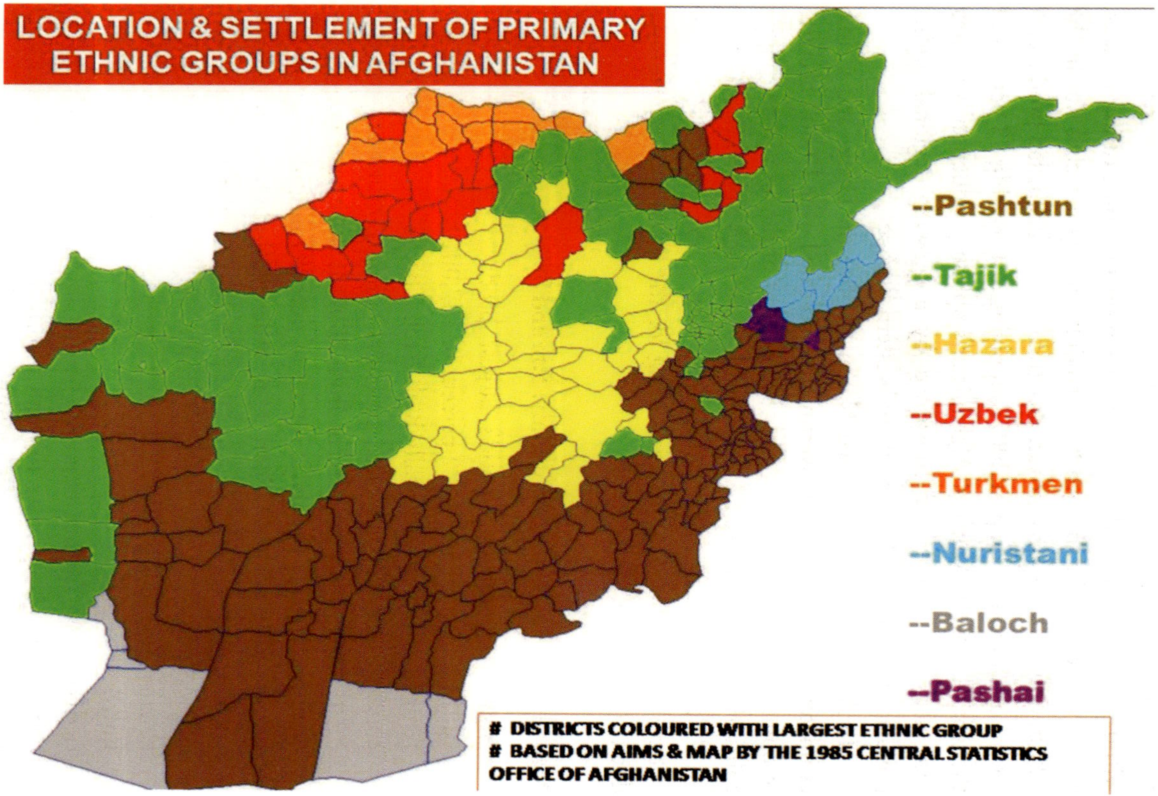
LOCATION & SETTLEMENT OF PRIMARY ETHNIC GROUPS IN AFGHANISTAN
--Pashtun
--Tajik
--Hazara
--Uzbek
--Turkmen
--Nuristani
--Baloch
--Pashai
DISTRICTS COLOURED WITH LARGEST ETHNIC GROUP
BASED ON AIMS & MAP BY THE 1985 CENTRAL STATISTICS OFFICE OF AFGHANISTAN

Opium has become a ready source of cash for many Afghans, especially following the breakdown in central authority after the Soviet withdrawal and opium-derived revenues probably constituting a major source of income for the two main factions during the civil war in the 1990s. Opium is easy to cultivate and transport. Afghanistan produced a record opium poppy crop in 2007, supplying a staggering 93 percent of the world's opium. Much of Afghanistan's opium production is refined into heroin and is either consumed by a growing regional addict population or exported, primarily to Western Europe.

In August 2007, the United Nations Office on Drugs and Crime estimated that the Afghan Government eradicated over 19,000 hectares of opium poppy, representing only 9.9 percent of the area under poppy cultivation. The year 2004 witnessed a historic high opium-poppy crop of 206,700 hectares under cultivation, with 4,950 metric tonnes of potential opium production accounting for the majority of the world's illicit opium supply.

Afghanistan's illicit opium economy: Size and Shape

- Afghanistan remains world's largest producer of opium. Poppy cultivation decreased by 22 percent to 157,000 hectares in 2008 but remains still at a historically high level. The less favorable growing conditions in 2008 reduced potential opium production to 5,500 metric tons, down 31 percent from 2007. If the entire opium crop were processed, 648 metric tonnes of pure heroin potentially could be produced. The Taliban and other anti-government groups participate in and profit from the opiate trade, which is a key source of revenue for the Taliban inside Afghanistan. Widespread corruption and instability impede counter-drug efforts. It should be noted that most of the heroin consumed in Europe and Eurasia is derived from Afghan opium. There is increasing vulnerability to drug money laundering through informal financial networks and regional source of 'hashish' (2008).
- From 1996 to 1999, under the Taliban, production doubled and peaked at over 4600 tons. In 2000 the Taliban banned opium cultivation, but not trade. By 2000, the country was the source of 70

percent of all illicit opium produced in the world. Following a decline in 2001, production resumed at high levels in 2002, again making Afghanistan the world's largest producer (followed by Myanmar and Laos), accounting for almost three-quarters of global opium production. Afghanistan's opium production (3400 tons in 2002) increased more than 15-fold since 1979 when the Soviets invaded Afghanistan. Opium was being cultivated by several ethnic groups in the south (Helmand), east (Nangrahar) and north (Badakshan). Cross-border ethnic and tribal links facilitate trafficking by several ethnic groups. Over three-quarters of the heroin sold in Europe, and virtually all of it in Russia, originates in Afghanistan.

- During the 19th century and early 20th century, one of the main opium production centres of the country was Badakshan (northern Afghanistan), known for its high-quality opium. However, the subsequent expansion of opium production, notably the expansion in the 1980s and the 1990s took place mainly in the east and in the 1990s, in the south of the country. By the year 2000, before the Taliban ban, the two provinces, Helmand (southern Afghanistan) and Nangrahar (eastern Afghanistan) accounted for slightly more than 75 percent of the total area under poppy cultivation (51.9 percent and 23.9 percent respectively). The area under cultivation in Badakshan was 3 percent of the country's total poppy cultivation. Cultivation in Badakshan rose by 43 percent between the period 1994-2000, though rising from low levels. The strongest decline in absolute terms over the same period was reported from the province of Nangrahar (-32 percent in relative terms).
- The basic regional trends over the 1994-2000 period were thus a decline of production in the East of Afghanistan, but strong increases in the South as well as in the North of the country. The opium poppy ban decreed by the Taliban in July 2000 led to massive declines of between 90 percent and 100 percent of cultivation in the provinces controlled by them in 2001. Cultivation in Helmand ceased entirely and cultivation in Nangrahar fell by 99 percent. Increases were only reported from two Northern provinces,

Badakshan (+158 percent) and Samangan (+1,037 percent). In the other Northern provinces cultivation fell as well. A decline of two thirds was reported in Takhar, which neighbours Badakshan, as well as an almost complete elimination in Kunduz and Balkh, the two provinces neighbouring Samangan.

- The main Northern provinces (Badakshan, Samangan, Takhar, Balkh) were responsible for almost 95 percent of Afghanistan's opium poppy cultivation in 2001. Most of the rest, close to 5 percent, was produced in Eastern Afghanistan (Nangrahar, Kunar, Kabul, Laghman, Paktia). Southern Afghanistan virtually ceased to be an opium production area. Nonetheless, in some of the key opium producing provinces, opium poppy cultivation reached significant proportions. In Nangrahar more than a fifth of arable land (22 percent) was used for poppy cultivation in 2002, and around 17 percent of arable land in Uruzgan and Helmand (southern Afghanistan) were used for such cultivation. In Badakshan, the respective proportion was 8 percent in 2002. The provinces of Kunar and Laghman in the East and Kandahar in the South were also clearly above the overall average of 0.9 percent. The regional concentration of opium poppy cultivation becomes even morc apparent when cultivation of opium poppy is compared to the cultivation of Afghanistan's main agricultural cropwheat.
- In Nangrahar the area under poppy was equivalent to almost 60 percent of the land under wheat cultivation in 2002. In Helmand the corresponding ratio was 48 percent. In Badakshan and Uruzgan the area under opium poppy cultivation was equivalent to 15 percent of the area under wheat cultivation. Proportions ranging from 1 percent 10 percent were reported from Kunar, Ghor, Kandahar, Laghman, Kapisa and Nimroz. Overall the highest concentrations of opium poppy as compared to wheat production were found in eastern Afghanistan, followed by southern Afghanistan.
- The area under poppy cultivation is a tiny fraction of the arable land in Afghanistan (0.9 percent in 2002). Even in the poppy growing villages, only 8 percent of the arable land was used for opium cultivation in 2000, though in Helmand and Nangrahar the rates were significantly higher (about one-third of arable land). Today, the

bulk of poppy cultivation again takes place on irrigated land in the south, where productivity can be 3-4 times higher than in the rain-fed provinces of the north. Most ethnic groups are involved in opium production though there seems to be a concentration between Pashtun and Tajik villages located in the main opium producing regions of southern, eastern and northern Afghanistan.

Trade and Income

- Over the 1994-2000 period, gross income from opium was about $150 million/year ($750/family). The opium trade was de-facto legal in Afghanistan before and throughout the Taliban period. Opium farm gate prices increased almost 10-fold ($300 per kg) at harvest time in 2001 compared to a year earlier as a consequence of the Taliban opium ban and some 20- fold ($700 kg) prior to September 11, 2001. In 2001 following the Taliban ban, prices increased 10-fold. Opium markets in southern Afghanistan were fragmented and competitive, while in the east and north they were oligopolistic. Price levels and structures varied accordingly, but they are now converging. Income from opium and heroin trafficking into neighbouring countries amounted to at least $720 million in 2000. It may have doubled in 2002. In 2002, gross income rose to $1.2 billion ($6,500/family). Part of the income was shared with traders and/or taxed by warlords. These are extraordinary revenues in a country where the average wage does not exceed $2 per day. In January 2002, the Karzai Administration banned it.

Drug Abuse

- Drug abuse in Afghanistan has increased strongly in the last few years, due to prolonged human deprivation and suffering, the breakdown of traditional social controls, the return of refugees who developed a drug problem in refugee camps and the almost unlimited availability of opiates within Afghanistan. The war wounded also became addicted as consequence of primitive first aid and large-scale use of opium, morphine, and heroin as painkillers.

Drug abuse in Afghanistan is still low compared to neighbouring countries (Iran, Pakistan, and Central Asia).

- Afghanistan has begun its counter-narcotics programmes, including the promotion of alternative livelihoods, public information campaigns, targeted eradication policies, interdiction of drug shipments, as well as law enforcement and justice reform programmes. In fact, these programmes were first implemented in late 2005.

Poverty, Devastation and Farmers' motivations

Afghan farmers grew opium poppy due to numerous factors. The opium trade was de-facto legal until President Karzai's ban in January 2002. Opium poppy is a profitable crop, produced with cheap labour that includes women, children and refugees. Inputs for opium poppy are abundant, including suitable land, water and know-how from itinerant labor. Opium became a form of saving, a source of liquidity and a collateral for credit. Opium is an insurance against poverty and hunger. Farmers sell future crops to narco-users for subsistence and opium requires no marketing or storage since it can be sold easily on spot markets.

Bazaars, Finance and Narco-Usurers (Money Lenders)

Opium has become an "economic narcotic" for wholesome segments of the Afghan society. As a commodity, it is an income generator. As a source of liquidity, it is a means of exchange. As a payment mechanism, it is a way to store value and fund transactions. Opium traders frequently act as narco-users because:

- Opium serves as a means of salaam (informal advance payments);
- They have capital to assist farmers. They regenerate cash-flows via rapid turnover trade (low profit); and
- Or via shipments to border regions (medium profit); or by smuggling opiates across borders (high profit). Thus the risks vary accordingly.

GREED, WARLORDS AND THE OPIUM TRADES

Opium is an ideal commodity for marketing, trade and speculation. It is compact to transport and durable to store, with high intrinsic value ($350-400/kg). At present, only a few licit agricultural commodities, such as truffles ($800/kg) are more expensive on international markets. Given high risk of interdiction at the borders with neighboring countries, high profits (five-fold increases of price) are generated by trafficking. It is a commodity suitable for trafficking, especially in the provinces controlled by warlords who levy a tax in exchange for protection. In some regions, traffickers gain respect from the local community when they recycle part of their income for the benefit of poor villages.

There is a clear nexus between drug trafficking and war-lordism. The re-emergence of drug cultivation and the recrudescence of violence in certain provinces are a well-known phenomena. The opium trade has evolved over the last two decades as a de-facto legal activity, to become an integral part of Afghanistan's war economy, with opium going out of the country and arms coming in. Smuggling of licit goods became another illegal pursuit supporting the war economy, chiefly as a result of the earlier (1950s) Afghan Transit Trade Agreement (ATTA) that enabled land-locked Afghanistan to import goods duty-free into the country via Pakistan.

Apart from supporting the central institutions of the state, the international support has to be targeted at solving the problems, which created the opium economy in the first place. Alternate crops, seeds, fertilizers and equipment for opium farmers, can solve the existing problems. Alternative sources of income for landless labour and returning refugees need to be sorted out. There should be focused efforts towards creation of jobs for women and schooling for children, especially girls. Macro-economic structures within which commodity markets (including presently unregulated bazaars) can grow free from the perverse incentives provided by opium and other forms of contraband. Informal financial structures able to extend harvest-based collateralized loans (even micro credits) to farmers and returning refugees, so as to bankrupt the narco-users at their game. Effective law enforcement against opium markets within the country to combat the perverse economic and political impact of warlordism and against the international trafficking of opiates.

TRADE AND INDUSTRY

For Afghanistan, the main regional players in terms of cross-border trade are Pakistan and Iran. Most of Afghanistan's external trade by land passes through the cities of Jalalabad and Herat and they have emerged as hubs of trade. Afghanistan is endowed with natural resources, including extensive deposits of natural gas, petroleum, coal, copper, chromite, talc, barites, sulfur, lead, zinc, iron ore, salt, and precious and semi-precious stones. The ongoing instability in certain areas of the country, remote and rugged terrain and an inadequate infrastructure and transportation network have made mining these resources difficult with few serious attempts to further explore or exploit them. The Ministry of Mines also forwarded oil, gas and iron ore tenders in 2008.

The most important resource has been natural gas, first tapped in 1967. At their peak during the 1980s, natural gas sales accounted for $300 million a year in export revenues (56 percent of the total). 90 percent of these exports went to the Soviet Union to pay for imports and debts. However, during the withdrawal of Soviet troops in 1989, Afghanistan's natural gas fields were capped to prevent sabotage by the mujahideen. Restoration of gas production has been hampered by internal strife and the disruption of traditional trading relationships following the collapse of the Soviet Union.

TRANSPORTATION

During the 1960s, the United States helped build a highway connecting Afghanistan's two largest cities. It began in Kabul and wound its way through five of the country's core provinces and eventually reaching Kandahar. More than 35 percent of the country's population lives within 50 kilometers of this highway, called, appropriately, modern Afghanistan's lifeline. In 1978, the Soviet Union invaded and after more than two decades of war, the Kabul-Kandahar highway was devastated, like much of the country's infrastructure. Restoration of the highway has been an overriding priority of the Karzai administration. Without the highway link, Afghanistan's civil society and economy would remain moribund and prey to divisive forces. The economic development that the highway makes possible will help guarantee the unity and long-term security of the Afghan people. The restored highway is a visually impressive achievement whose symbolic importance should not be underestimated. It marks a palpable transition from the recent past and represents an important building block for the future.

The highway will not end in Kandahar, there are plans to complete the circuit, extending it to Herat and then arching it back through Mazar-e-Sharif to Kabul. The route is sometimes referred to as the Ring Road. As of December 2006, 100 percent of the Ring Road had been funded, with plans for completion in 2009-10. Civil aviation has been expanding rapidly and several private airlines now offer an alternative to Ariana and operate a domestic and international route network. Many sections of Afghanistan's highway and regional road system are undergoing significant reconstruction, many with substantial Americans assistance. The Asian Development Bank is also active in road development projects, mainly in the border areas with Pakistan.

In early 2003, Iran concluded a number of trade agreements with Afghanistan, enticing Kabul to use its Chabahar port on Indian Ocean as an alternative to the southern Pakistani port of Karachi, which has served as a traditional transit route for Afghanistan. India bankrolled the development of the Chabahar port and major road projects to aid the transformation. Meanwhile, Pakistan built a new seaport in Gwadar a few hundred kilometers south of Chabahar. Built with major Chinese investment, the port will also serve as a major hub for the rapidly growing trade and industry in western Chinese regions bordering Pakistan.

DE-MINING

Afghanistan is one of the most heavily mined countries in the world; an estimated 200,000 Afghans have been disabled by the explosive remnants of war (ERW). Between March 2006 and March 2007, an average 62 civilians were injured each month. As of March 2007 the United Nations

Mine Action Program for Afghanistan (MAPA), responsible for demining in Afghanistan, employed approximately 8,500 Afghan personnel through funding and oversight of several non-governmental organizations (NGOs) deployed throughout the country. With support from the Afghanistan government and in line with its Ottawa Convention commitments, MAPA has destroyed Afghanistan's known stockpile of landmines and strives to make Afghanistan mine-free by 2013.

Since 1989, MAPA has cleared about 1.2 billion square meters of land and destroyed millions of ERW, including over 300,000 anti-personnel landmines. Training programmes are also provided to educate the public about the threat and dangers of ERW. These combined efforts have reduced ERW victims by over 50 percent in the past six years.

INDIA'S INVESTMENT IN AFGHANISTAN

Afghanistan should be viewed as a fast growing emerging market of strategic importance, close to some of the largest and fastest-growing markets in the world. The country offers a pro-business minded environment with legislation favorable to private investments and is rich in natural resources. Afghanistan has been finalized as the eighth member of SAFTA. As member of SAFTA, Afghanistan will receive the benefit of zero import duty by India on 4536 tariff lines. Currently, under the Preferential Trade Arrangement (PTA) with Afghanistan, the rules of origin stipulate 50 percent domestic value addition for export within the South Asian region. As Afghanistan comes under the SAFTA fold, this would come down to 30 percent. This indeed should be viewed as a significant step for the Afghan economy and help boost its exports to India. As against US $ 400 million total FDI into Afghanistan in 2006-07, India's share was a mere $10 million. Indian companies should make pro-active investments for the development of the Afghan economy.

Trade and investment linkages between India and Afghanistan are expected to further deepen and India-Afghan trade would rise from $ 216 million in 2006-07 to $ 1 billion during the next five years. The total commitment of Indian investment for the reconstruction of the Afghan economy during the last five years stood at $ 750 million, making India the fifth largest development partner of Afghanistan. The rate of disbursement of investment was even more encouraging at 37 percent. This means that $ 250 million worth of investment had actually been disbursed. Given the political relations between the two countries, such development assistance is bound to increase in the coming future.

The key constraints for bilateral economic cooperation primarily have been the difficult law and order situation, limited trade basket between India and Afghanistan, lack of trade infrastructure and non-availability of skilled manpower in Afghanistan. India has in a major way taken up a non-military role in rebuilding Afghanistan by helping build roads, hospitals, schools and training bureaucracy and police. India's investment in the battle-torn country has already crossed $1.2 billion (about Rs 6,000 crore). Afghanistan has vast reserves of iron ore, thorium, gas, coal, copper and other minerals and it is about time that Indian business invests in the country should increase manifold times.

CHINESE INVESTMENT IN AFGHAN INDUSTRIES

China showed little interest in Afghanistan throughout the 20th century but its growing energy and natural resources demand combined with increasing Afghan openness to foreign investors have made Beijing of the country's leading trade partner. China remained disengaged in Afghanistan until the Karzai government opened up its energy, mineral and raw materials to foreign investors. The growing interest was particularly manifested during the first significant investment in the mining sector in Afghanistan that commenced in 2008 for the development of the Aynak copper field deposit in east-central Afghanistan. China's Metallurgical group won the bid to a $3.5 billion investment to develop Afghanistan's Aynak copper field situated in the Logar province—thus far the largest foreign direct investment in Afghanistan's history. Reports from Kabul also indicate that additional Chinese investments are underway.

The copper field is estimated to be the largest undeveloped field in the world and has been virtually untouched since the Soviet invasion in 1979. The investment involves not only mining but also the construction of a $500 million electrical plant and a railway from Tajikistan to

Pakistan to support exploration. The mine is expected to be fully operational, in around six years, providing to the employment of nearly 10,000 Afghans. It is expected to yield ... as royalty to $400 million Afghan government yearly—more than half of the present yearly state budget. The mine is also estimated to generate millions of dollars in taxes and $200 million in annual shareholder revenues. Furthermore, the shallow Aynak field is comparatively easy to develop, which speaks in favour of a fast materialization of this project.

The Chinese exploration of Aynak copper field in all likelihood is the start of Beijing's drive to seize as large a share as possible of Afghanistan's natural resources. The Chinese government likely is to be successful in these endeavors considering China's good standing in Afghanistan, ability to distort the market, and fiscal wherewithal to outbid its competitors.

According to estimates, the 28-square-kilometer copper field in Logar Province could contain up to $88 billion worth of ore. But there is no power plant in the area that can generate enough electricity for the mining and extraction operations. Additionally, Afghanistan has never had the kind of railroad needed to haul away tonnes of copper that could be extracted. That is why a large part of the Chinese bid includes the cost of building a 400-megawatt, coal-fired power plant and a freight railroad passing from western China through Tajikistan and Afghanistan to Pakistan. The extraction and production of copper begins with explosives. Then it is processed in a way that produces [toxic] dust and dangerous gasses—affecting areas near and far. Thus, concerns have been expressed about the need for the Chinese firm to prevent toxins from seeping into the underground water table. A vital apprehension is regarding the fact, that drinking-water supplies could be contaminated for people as far away as Kabul.

There are plenty of factors suggesting that China is set to increase its investments in Afghanistan in the near future. Afghanistan has unexplored reserves of oil and natural gas in the northern parts of the country. The Afghan oil reserves were recently upgraded 18 times by a US geological survey, estimates standing at a mean of 1,596 million barrels, while Afghanistan's natural gas reserves were upgraded by a factor of three, standing at a mean of 15,687 trillion cubic feet (tcf).

Afghanistan also possesses large iron ore deposits between Herat and the Panjsher Valley, and gold reserves in the northern provinces of Badakshan, Takhar and Ghazni. Major copper fields also exist in Jawkhar, Darband. All of these resource-rich areas are also situated in the relatively stable northern and northwestern regions. Moreover, China's iron-ore demand had increased close to 15 percent during the first half of 2007, while copper demand surged by almost 35 percent in the same period. Natural gas demand also increased rapidly and China continues to desperately seek overland energy supply diversification in the neighboring states in Central Asia and potentially also in Afghanistan.

The project contributes to Beijing's plans for the development of western China and its regional trade links. In order to develop the west [of China], they need energy resources and they need other resource materials. So far, Afghanistan has remained virtually untouched by Beijing's concerns, in contrast to China's involvement in Central Asia, Pakistan, and Iran. "The past few years have seen investments into the Karakoram Highway in Pakistan, the Gwadar port (in Karachi), and a multibillion-dollar pipeline from Kazakhstan to Xinjiang (Uyghur Autonomous Region.) Understandably, this of course constitutes a part of the greater strategy.

Besides, Chinese companies ZTE and Huawei partnered with the Afghan Ministry of Communications have collaborated to implement digital telephone switches, providing roughly 200,000 subscriber lines. China is also contributing in the Parwan irrigation project, restoring water supply in Parwar province, as well as reconstruction of the public hospitals in Kabul and Kandahar. Moreover, the EU has hired Chinese firms for various construction projects in Afghanistan, including road restoration activities.

RISK ASSESSMENT

Unrelenting Structural Weaknesses: The economy slumped in 2008-09 as a result of relatively poorer harvests, a shortage of rain, and upward price pressure associated with the rise of raw material prices. Economic growth remained nonetheless strong, driven by massive investments by foreign donors and buoyant private consumption, spurred in part by large earnings linked to illegal opium poppy harvests.

In 2009-10, growth may accelerate slightly amid easing inflation. Several factors continue to limit GDP growth, however, including persistent political uncertainties, deficient infrastructure (particularly for electricity), and a developed narcotics economy with the opium poppy the country's most important crop and opium production growing rapidly. In 2008, Afghanistan produced 93 per cent of the world opium supply up from 52 per cent in 1995. The underground opium economy has a substantial impact on the Afghan growth—it siphons off 12 percent of the population in the legitimate labour market and its production represents $ 1 billion, or 11 percent of total licit GDP. Opium trafficking moreover tends to spawn widespread corruption and enhance the power of complicit local tribal leaders.

Afghanistan continues to depend on massive international aid. Large official transfers and partial debt relief under the HIPC programme have, however, facilitated improvement in financial ratios—a trend that is likely to continue in 2009-10.

The political context in the run-up to presidential elections remains extremely precarious. The central government has struggled to impose its authority in many provincial areas. The NATO and ISAF forces continue to experience difficulties in retaking areas under Taliban's control in the south. The direction that Afghanistan is likely to take after the presidential elections in 2009 remains a major uncertainty as the incumbent president, Hamid Karzai, although legally qualified to run, lacks broad support in the country.

REFERENCES

1. For more details see, *CIA World Fact book,* Profile of Afghanistan, 2009.
2. Statistics obtained by a survey in Afghanistan by UNICEF and *World Health Report,* 2003.
3. *UNHCR Statistical Yearbook 2006,* (Geneva: UNHCR, December 2007), p. 36; also see, 2007 *Global Trends: Refugees, Asylum-seekers, Returnees, Internally Displaced and Stateless Persons* (Geneva: UNHCR, June 2008), pp. 8-9.

4. *Ibid.*
5. Adam B. Ellick, "Afghan Refugees Return Home, but Find Only a Life of Desperation," *New York Times,* December 2, 2008; Figure for internally displaced persons from *Economic and Social Rights Report in Afghanistan - III* (Kabul: Afghanistan Independent Human Rights Commission, December 2008), p. 49.
6. Adam Roberts, "Doctrine and Reality in Afghanistan," *Survival,* vol. 51, no. 1, February-March 2009, p. 30.
7. *Ibid.*
8. Ahmed Rashid, *Taliban: The Story of the Afghan Warlords,* (London: Pan Books, 2001), pp. 11724.
9. US Department of State, *Background Note - Afghanistan,* November 2008.
10. Report by the United Nations Office on Drugs and Crime, *"The Opium Economy in Afghanistan: An International Problem,"* January 2003.
11. US Department of State, Country Background, *Afghanistan,* October 2008.
12. *Ibid.*
13. *Ibid.*
14. Adam B. Ellick, "Afghan Refugees Return Home, but Find Only a Life of Desperation," *New York Times,* December 2, 2008; Figure for internally displaced persons from *Economic and Social Rights Report in Afghanistan - III* (Kabul: Afghanistan Independent Human Rights Commission, December 2008), p. 49.
15. Adam Roberts, "Doctrine and Reality in Afghanistan," *Survival,* vol. 51, no. 1, February-March 2009, p. 30.
16. *Ibid.*
17. Ahmed Rashid, *Taliban: The Story of the Afghan Warlords,* (London: Pan Books, 2001), pp. 11724.
18. US Department of State, *Background Note - Afghanistan,* November 2008.
19. Report by the United Nations Office on Drugs and Crime, *"The Opium Economy in Afghanistan: An International Problem,"* January 2003.
20. US Department of State, Country Background, *Afghanistan,* October 2008.
21. *Ibid.*

5

Afghanistan—Stake Holders Analysis: USA, EU, Russia, India, Iran, China, Central Asian States and Pakistan

INTRODUCTION

Stake holder analysis is a qualitative technique which provides a detailed review of stakes of various parties correlated to interests of the principal. Afghanistan is in the sway of multiple conflicts of varying hues, state stability, terrorism, drug proliferation, proxy war and so on. The country is also on the geographical fault lines in Asia between West-South and Central Asia and has a long legacy of conflicts. Thus there are multiple players involved in Afghanistan with varied interests frequently clashing with each other adding to existing acrimony.

Indian interests in Afghanistan are linked to the overall objective of regional peace and stability. While on the whole this is congruent with other stake holders, yet conflicting interests has resulted in a debate on the scope and limitations of India's role in the country. Stakeholder analysis can thus provide an overview of varied perspectives by parties in Afghanistan and how it impacts Indian interests. This can in turn help us shape not just the policy in Afghanistan but also overall bilateral and multilateral engagement with specific reference to this as well as other related issues. This approach can also help us develop and implement a strategic communication and advocacy campaign. This is also a tool for policymakers and managers to assess, interests, positions and alliances thereby facilitating effective engagement in support of our policy therein. Thus, a detailed stake holder analysis of Afghanistan with reference to in the pages that follow in this chapter.

GENERAL

The Process of Stake Holder Analysis: Stakeholder analysis involves systematic collection and analysis of qualitative information to determine the interests of various players that need to be taken into account when developing and/or implementing a policy or program. Stakeholders in this case are states with a interest in the policy being promoted. The analysis will include such stakeholder characteristics as interests related to general and India's policy, position for or against the same, potential alliances and ability to affect the policy process (through power and/or leadership). Stake holder analysis is aims to provide an understanding of who support and oppose India's policy or program and the degree of this support or opposition. The overall aim is to guide implementation of our policy or program.

INDIAN INTERESTS IN AFGHANISTAN

India's interests in Afghanistan have been outlined by Indian Ambassador Mr Jayant Prasad, thus, "Our strategic interest is very well served if there is peace and stability in Afghanistan. If Afghanistan has a functional government, democracy and pluralism, that return itself is good for India." These are also related to national goal and objectives indicated by the government from time to time. Afghanistan is a primary concern for India due to its impact on global and regional stability. The Af-Pak region is perceived as the base of global and regional terrorism with presence of international terrorist groups as the Al Qaeda, Taliban, Lashkar-e-Taiyyaba, Jaish e Mohammad and other UN proscribed non state actors as Jamaat ud Dawa.

Stability in Afghanistan fits in with the vision of a co-operative sub continent most recently flagged by the Indian Prime Minister in his remarks to the Press on 17 June thus, "I have spoken before of my vision of a co-operative subcontinent, and of the vital interest that India and the people of the subcontinent have in peace."

Mr Shiv Shankar Menon, former foreign secretary indicated that a stable Afghanistan also fits into foreign policy goals of the country of a peaceful periphery and good relations with neighbours, transformation of relations with major powers and working with the international community to see a rapid recovery of the world economy.

The tools for implementation of this policy are essentially economic aid and development assistance. The key to stability in Afghanistan is thus through capacity building of Afghan institutions in all spheres economic, security and governance. India has been contributing to the same in varying degrees based on firstly the demands made by the Afghan government and people and role deemed appropriate by the international community.

However, in the larger context there has been continued resistance by Pakistan to India's presence in Afghanistan and has been contesting the same in various forums from time to time. Pakistan has even adopted the asymmetric route of targeting Indian embassy in Kabul in July 2008 and October 2009 through its terrorist proxies. However there is strong support for Indian role in Afghanistan from the Afghan people as well as the international community which has sustained the commitment thus far. A stake holder analysis in the light of the above would provide greater clarity on the issue as is being carried out in subsequent paragraphs. India has vital security stakes in the stabilisation of a nation state in Afghanistan. In simple geostrategic terms, these can be outlined as under:

- In purely military terms, in the Soviet era, Afghanistan had tied down two Pakistani Corps on its western front. Post 1989, these became available to Pakistan for deployment against India. Pakistan's consequent perception of conventional military parity has encouraged her to launch the proxy war in J&K, and now a terrorist jihad in Indian cities. The destruction of the Afghan nation state has created the military resource surplus which has encouraged Pakistan to launch its asymmetric war of a thousand cuts against India.
- Afghanistan has traditionally been hostile to Pakistan on issues of the Durand Line's legality and access to the sea. This has served to put Pakistan in a classic two-front situation. India therefore has vital geopolitical stakes in the continued existence of a viable and independent Afghan state.
- The Afghan nation state was one of the oldest states of Asia. It became the first failed state in Asia. In the interests of regional

stability, this contagion of collapse must be contained. It must not be allowed to spread.

- As per Robert Gates, US Defence Secretary and former Director CIA, during the Taliban regime in Kabul (1996-2001), 22% of all terrorists operating in J&K were either from Afghanistan or had been trained there. *India therefore simply cannot afford to let Afghanistan be controlled or dominated by any power hostile to India.*
- A client regime of Pakistan in Kabul seriously curtails India's access to the hydro-carbon resources and markets of Central Asia.
- India can accept Taliban's resurgence in Afghanistan only at its own strategic peril. Even the "moderate Taliban" in Kabul could soon result in the Domino effect of the Talibanisation of Pakistan and later Central Asia. The systemic collapse of Pakistan could place Weapons of Mass Destruction (WMD) in the hands of Non-State Actors. This would have very serious implications not just for Indian Security but also the peace and stability of the existing global system *per se.*

STAKE HOLDER ANALYSIS

General: The level of stakes of a country in Afghanistan can be determined as vital, high, medium and low and in terms of primary or secondary interest. Stake holder analysis is generally relevant of those players who have high to medium stakes which in this case include the United States, European Union, Russia, China, Iran, Pakistan, Central Asia and finally Afghanistan as being carried out as per subsequent paragraphs.

USA

As the primary global power, despite diffusion in the recent past, the United States remains the key player in Afghanistan. Washington has a high stake in Afghanistan and the country is of primary interest. US goals and objectives in Afghanistan have been very succinctly indicated by Secretary of State Hillary Clinton at the Council for Foreign Relations in Washington and links Afghanistan to Pakistan thus, "In Afghanistan and

Pakistan, our goal is to disrupt, dismantle, and ultimately defeat al-Qaida and its extremist allies, and to prevent their return to either country. To achieve our goals, President Obama is sending an additional 17,000 troops and 4,000 military trainers to Afghanistan. Equally important, we are sending hundreds of 'direct hire American civilians' to lead a new effort to strengthen the Afghan Government, help rebuild the once-vibrant agricultural sector, create jobs, encourage the rule of law, expand opportunities for women, and train the Afghan police. No one should doubt our commitment to Afghanistan and its people. But it is the Afghan people themselves who will determine their own future." The Af-Pak plan outlined by President Obama had lowered the bar to simply eliminating the Al Qaeda, and thereby left scope to strike a deal with the so called Moderate Taliban. This is being seen as part of an exit strategy from Afghanistan. The original plan is now being modified to a more Pak-Af orientation, with a much higher emphasis on saving the state of Pakistan. There is concerted debate in the USA whether the battle in Afghanistan is worth the fight, and whether it would be feasible or advisable for the US and it allies to attempt armed nation building in a state which has traditionally been the graveyard of empires.

The US Policy in Afghanistan to achieve the goals and objectives stated above as outlined by President Obama includes the following key features:

- A Regional Approach.
- Building Capacity and More Training of the Afghan National Army and Police
- Using All Elements of National Power including civilian effort in governance
- Bringing new international elements to the effort.

A review of the current strategy has been undertaken by US commander in Afghanistan, Lt General McChrystal and refinement is due in the rules of engagement without altering the basic tenets outlined by President Obama.

On the whole battling extremism represented by the Al Qaeda and the Taliban is important to the United States. While in the larger context of geopolitics, a strategic presence in South West Asia provides it access to Central Asia, China and Russia on one hand and Iran and West Asia on the other. The United States is also looking at curtailing the drug route emanating from Afghanistan and spanning the Islamic crescent. These are its primary stakes.

Secondary stakes include enhancing economic profile in the region particularly through development projects, sale of arms and equipment and also accessing strategic minerals in Afghanistan and Central Asia. The short term objective of the United States is primarily denial of base for terrorism, ensuring stability and denial of access of nuclear weapons of Pakistan to the terrorist groups. The US infrastructure in the Afghan air bases is being built for the long haul. It is likely that the USA would like to retain a greatly reduced ground footprint that is offset by employing airpower and Special Forces in an over watch role. It is therefore likely, that President Obama could declare victory by 2011 (before the next US Presidential Elections) and pull out the bulk of ground troops. However, should Vice President Joe Biden's plan be accepted over the proposals submitted by Lt Gen McChrystal (for a further troop surge of 40,000-60,000) then the thinning out of the US ground forces presence could commence much earlier in Afghanistan (as early as 2010).

In the context of Indian interests in Afghanistan there is a congruence, yet the United States is constrained by regional politics of Indo Pakistan and Indo China contestations particularly the former. Thus while accepting India's primarily role in the region, the US would attempt to shape the same in a manner that is acceptable to Pakistan. The US also sees India as a hedging power in South West Asia in the light of its relationship with Russia, China and Iran which would be determined by the way Indo US relationship shape up. At present this issue is best left open ended.

India needs to leverage commonality of threats emanating from Islamic extremism in the region and its manifestation the Al Qaeda and particularly the Lashkar-e-Taiyyaba-Jaish combination which is increasingly attaining a global profile and would therefore be important to neutralize with its base in the Af-Pak region. This would have to be subtly incorporated in Indian engagement with the United States.

EUROPEAN UNION/NATO

By its active involvement in Afghanistan's security and aid and development, the European Union through its extension NATO has medium stakes in Afghanistan and its interests appear secondary in nature, given that these are in tandem with the need to maintain solidarity with the United States and traditional western alliance as such. Afghanistan is also seen by the EU as a test bed for its Eurasia policy extending from the European to the Asian theatre. This will provide it access to Central Asia and China, Iran and West Asia, however the most important aspect is EU's relationship with Russia. Here a balance of power is emerging where EU states would like to see Afghanistan policy as a tool for leveraging relations with Moscow.

The EU is also increasingly concerned of the rise in Islamic extremism and thus destruction of the Al Qaeda and the Taliban would be of interest to the EU. Countries as Britain have a sizeable Islamic population from the Sub Continent particularly from Pakistan and are thus sensitive to the rise of fundamentalism. Drugs are another concern with the flow making increasing impact on the youth in Europe.

At another level EU countries are keen to expand their economic profile not just through aid and development but also through various infrastructure projects, sale of arms and equipment and access to strategic minerals in Afghanistan and Central Asia. The short term objectives would thus include solidarity with the United States; here intensity of engagement would differ to the degree of unity each country seeks with Washington, with older Europe being less rather than more engaged. Containing proliferation of drugs and denial of base to terror would remain the key short term goals.

Former Danish prime minister Anders Fogh Rasmussen took charge of the 28-nation NATO alliance in August. He highlighted that the long-term goal of the organisation was to "move forward concretely and visibly with transferring lead security responsibility in Afghanistan to the

Afghans," and "denied there was any move to cut and run." However European democracies will come under pressure from the people as casualties mount and this assertion may well change accordingly which needs consideration.

Given that EU policy towards Indian interests would be largely dictated by US perception, a calibrated acceptance of Indian engagement in Afghanistan is envisaged in tune with Washington.

RUSSIA

Afghanistan is a legacy of not just the Soviet engagement in the 1980's but also the Great Game of the 19th Century for Russia. Thus Russian policy is nuanced to denote avoidance of another setback. Russian stakes are low to medium and its interests seem to be secondary, though there are indications that Moscow may upgrade the same depending upon the emerging dynamics in the region. The trilateral and quadrilateral summits that Moscow has been having with Afghanistan, Pakistan and Tajikistan of late are a part of this shift the manifestations of which are still unclear. Thus an up-gradation of Russian interests and correspondingly stakes in Afghanistan from secondary to primary and from low to medium cannot be ruled out. In fact Russia is increasingly becoming a player in this region again. It has consolidated its influence in the Central Asian states and is now increasingly engaging Afghanistan. In fact it has been warming up to the Karzai regime and has recently provided US$100 million worth of arms to Kabul.

Russian interests in Afghanistan therefore relate to the strategic standoff with the United States over issues as presence in Central Asia, Georgia and Missile Defence. Moscow would like to leverage the same to its own advantage by providing logistics access to lethal and non lethal supplies. With Europe and NATO, Afghanistan once again provides a bargaining chip over expansion in the East and Eurasia policy. Increasingly stemming the Chinese influence in Central Asia is a concern for Russia and it has in the past upgraded its presence in the Shanghai Cooperation Organisation (SCO) which was being seen as a tool for Beijing to move west wards into Central Asia.

Russia remains concerned about the spread of Wahabi fundamentalism into Central Asia and its own Islamic underbelly in the Caucasus. It is equally concerned about the spread of narcotics from the Golden Crescent and the destabilizing impact of narco-terrorism upon Central Asia and the Caucasus region. It is noteworthy that there has been a spillover of terrorist activities in the Fergana valley and Tajikistan. Russia has steadily regained its influence in the Central Asian region. It has successfully bargained with the Americans to provide logistics support and supply routes for US/NATO forces in Afghanistan. The US has been forced to make concessions over Georgia and on the issue of basing anti-ballistic missile batteries in Poland and other east European states. Russia has quietly begun to reassert itself in Afghanistan. It has already offered US$100 million worth of arms and equipment to the Karzai regime in Kabul. It would therefore be in India's interest to closely coordinate its actions and responses in Afghanistan with Russians.

Russia would be supportive of Indian role in Afghanistan. However, to what extent it would aggressively sponsor the same would depend upon relative leverages that it has developed in the region over the years and as the prevailing situation.

CHINA

China's policy on Afghanistan is difficult to decipher. However it is fairly clear that China has medium stakes in Afghanistan and this is of secondary interest to Beijing, but is likely to increase with the flow of extremism from Afghanistan-Pakistan to Xingjian. The July 2009 ethnic riots are likely to have a spin off in rise of militancy in Chinas' Western province and Beijing is likely to be more sensitive to the role of Islamic extremism. Here China has adopted a pragmatic policy of avoiding confrontation with groups as the Taliban in the past and a strategic compromise is evident and China has remained out of the circle of targets identified by the Al Qaeda and Taliban so far. The Al Qaeda in the Maghreb in Algeria has recently announced intent to target Chinese workers and assets in that country, if these threats are carried out; China would review its policies but is unlikely to get into a major confrontation with the Al Qaeda or Taliban outside its own territory.

The strategic presence of the United States and EU in its close proximity is also likely to be a concern for the Chincse though this aspect remains unstatcd. China like Russia would also be concerned of the possible adverse spin offs from Af-Pak balkanisation if the situation comes to that pass.

China's main interests, as is evident at present are economic. China has developed primary stakes in minerals and mining in Afghanistan with a $3 billion project in Aynak copper mines in Logar near Kabul. Beijing with its penchant for large projects and ability to competitively bid for the same with geographical proximity will engage Afghanistan more deeply in the days ahead. In the short term with the need to prevent ingress of influence of Islamic extremism in Xingjian and in the long term for its economic interests China would support stability in Afghanistan.

China would not favour a larger Indian role in Afghanistan. While it may not seem to be directly against Indian involvement, any attempts to enlarge the profile would be resisted directly or through its proxy, Pakistan. This would be in line with the overall Chinese policy of containment of India in the region apart from supporting its strategic partner, Pakistan.

IRAN

As an immediate neighbour of Afghanistan as well as Pakistan Iran has vital stakes in its Eastern neighbour and thus the country is of primary interest to it. There are a number of issues of Iranian concern; such as presence of the Al Qaeda and the Taliban with Iran's sectarian difference apart from past legacy of conflict. In the Islamic ideological context battling Sunni extremism is a key concern for Iran. With a policy of proselytisation and enhancing linkages with Shia communities' worldwide, Iran could be well looking for a larger presence in Afghanistan as it would provide access to Central Asian Islamic countries as well. The strategic presence of the US in South West Asia is also a major worry for Iran given its long term conflict with the United States.

Iran is also keen to enhance its economic and trade profile in the region and would see Afghanistan as a corridor to Central Asia. Other key issue is of settlement of displaced persons from Afghanistan which are still camping in Iran and settlement of the border dispute that it has along the Helmand Valley. It is noteworthy that, Iran is deeply concerned about the security of the Hazara Shia groups in Afghanistan. The Taliban's massacre of the Hazaras and Uzbeks in 1997-98 almost led to a full scale war between Iran and the Taliban. Recently the Jundollah's terrorist attacks upon the Revolutionary Guard Commander of Sistan (the Baluch province of Iran) have evoked a sharp reaction from Iran. Iran has accused the ISI of fomenting this attack and supporting Jundollah insurgents in its territory.

Iran would be largely supportive of an Indian role in Afghanistan, whereas for India, Tehran remains the only access route to Kabul via the Persian Gulf. Thus for any larger engagement in Afghanistan, support of Iran is of vital importance for New Delhi. Unfortunately the imperatives of the Indo-US nuclear deal and India's import of arms from Israel have vitiated relations between India and Iran. India's vote against Iran in the IAEA contributed to the cooling of relations. India lost considerable traction in Iran to China which cornered most of the prized deals for the supply of LNG and the development of the Yedavaran oil fields. China's gains have been at India's costs. With the Indo-US Nuclear deal now sealed, India must reopen its bridges with Iran. Since the US itself is seeking a détente with Iran, India must seize the opportunity to refurbish its relations with this strategically vital country. Iran provides over 11% of India's oil imports and could be a lucrative source of natural gas. Iran also provides the only access routes to Afghanistan and Central Asia via its ports of Bander Abbas and Chabahar. In fact India has virtually no military options in Afghanistan unless it gets access via Iran. Iran is equally concerned about the possible resurgence of the Taliban in Afghanistan, and is likely to cooperate with India as it had done so earlier. Like Myanmar, India must not lose this vital state to China. There is an urgent need therefore for India to repair and strengthen its relationship with Iran.

PAKISTAN

Pakistan has long seen Afghanistan as an extension of its area of influence from the early 1980's with Soviet intervention in the country, where

Pakistan was the front line state for the Mujahideen and the later symbiotic relationship with the Taliban, Islamabad sees vital stakes in Afghanistan and it is of primary interest to it. Thus, Afghanistan forms the core of the strategic depth theory one of the primary considerations in Pakistan's national security discourse. The rise of Pakhtoon nationalism is another worry for Pakistan and Afghan rejection of the Durand Line is a matter of great concern for Islamabad. While it rejects the Balkanisation theory, with spread of militancy in the tribal areas, North West Frontier Province and Balochistan, Afghanistan is of vital importance to Pakistan. It is the cornerstone of its security as well as foreign policy.

Pakistan has also borne the burden of a large number of refugees though in turn it has developed vested interests with inflow of uncontrolled funds and human base for spreading extremist ideology, this has been used as a strategic resource over the years. On the positive side, it is also conscious of the enormous trade and transit benefits that Afghanistan would provide with access Central Asia and a transit and trade treaty is in the offing, but it is the negative spiral of strategic depth that continues to dominate Pakistani thinking.

Pakistan's short term objective would be to obtain maximum benefit from engagement of the international community in Afghanistan through aid and military support and continue a dominant influence over Afghanistan.

Pakistan is downright hostile to Indian presence in any form, for it sees a possible Indo Afghan coalition building up against its interests. Moreover, Afghanistan is also seen in a secular Islamic framework replicating India rather than a fundamentalist Islamic image in its own mould. These are factors which are generating insecurity in Pakistan and would therefore drive it to oppose any role for New Delhi in the welfare of its Western neighbour.

CENTRAL ASIAN REPUBLICS

The Central Asian Republics of Kazakhstan, Tajikistan and Kyrgyzstan have calibrated their stakes in Afghanistan in line with that of Russia.

However the danger of Islamic extremism emanating from the Af-Pak region with organisations as Islamic Mujahideen of Uzbekistan(IMU) has brought home the crisis nearer to the states of the Ferghana Valley. Afghanistan provides routes for trade to South and South East Asia as well as Japan in the East. Central Asian republics would therefore be supportive of Indian role and interests in Afghanistan. The Central Asian states, primarily Tajikistan and Uzbekistan were highly supportive of India's efforts to shore up the Northern Alliance. Tajikistan in fact had gone to the extent of providing an air base to India, as also permission to set up military hospitals to assist the Northern Alliance. Uzbekistan was the prime base and supply route for the Soviet forces in Afghanistan. Central Asian support would therefore be very useful to India for carrying out capacity building of the Afghan state. Military training infrastructure to train the ANA and its Air Corps could be set up in Tajkistan/Uzbekistan. All these Central Asian states are highly worried about the spread of Islamic fundamentalism from Afghanistan. The spillover effect is already visible in the revival of Islamic insurgencies in Tajikistan and the Fergana valley of Uzbekistan. India therefore needs to orchestrate a regional response to the problems of Afghanistan that must take on board Russia, Iran and the Central Asian states.

AFGHANISTAN

Afghanistan is largely supportive of Indian role and interests in the region. Over the years there is a symbiotic relationship that has grown between India and post Taliban Afghanistan. There are multiple fields of engagement, infra structure, development, aid, economy, trade and so on with a small military training component which has matured over the years. There is a genuine spirit of engagement in both the countries. Thus Mr Abdullah Abdullah a Presidential candidate for the elections in August 2009 says, "I think India is playing a very constructive role. It has contributed to the construction in Afghanistan. India is a not a donor country. Look at the contributions it has made and how it has helped and (in terms of) improvement in the life of the Afghan people in different ways and means." Establishment of Indo Afghanistan Partnership Council during July 2009 has added to growing proximity.

However, Afghanistan is also deeply conscious of antagonism that exists in the sub continent and has thus adopted a nuanced approach of engaging India taking into account sensitivities of Pakistan which is a pragmatic position which is well appreciated by New Delhi given the larger context in which it sees a partnership emerging with Kabul.

STAKE HOLDER AND ROLE CONGRUENCE MATRIX

Based on the above analysis a stake holder matrix is being attempted qualifying the states as supportive, selectively supportive, neutral or antagonist to Indian role and interests in Afghanistan as given below.

Supportive Russia Iran Central Asian States	**Selective Support** United States
Neutral/Varying Support European Union	**Antagonist** Pakistan China

An Indian role and policy congruence matrix based on the above analysis with respect to supportive or opposing states is as given below:

Factor	Supportive	Opposing	Undecided or Not Known
Economic Aid	All players less Pakistan and China	Pakistan	China
Development	All players less Pakistan and China	Pakistan	China
Civil Governance and other training	All players less Pakistan and China	Pakistan	China
Military Presence	Nill	US, Pakistan, China, EU	Afghanistan, Russia Iran
Military Training	US, EU, Afghanistan	Pakistan, China	Russia, Iran

CONCLUSIONS FROM STAKE HOLDER ANALYSIS

Key conclusions from the stake holder analysis above would indicate that there is broad support for Indian role and interests in Afghanistan but for rabid opposition from Pakistan and inferred resistance from China. The level of support varies but is largely related to economic aid and development assistance as well as military training. There is no country as of now which has supported or sought to support an Indian military role in Afghanistan.

India would therefore have to calibrate its goals and engagement in the region accordingly. The Afghans themselves are largely supportive of Indian role in the country; however it is not clear if they would welcome Indian military presence given its larger implications of relationship with Pakistan. Thus a nuanced approach would have to be adopted in Indo-Afghan engagement keeping in view India's overall regional interests and the possible collaborative or confrontationist approach likely to be adopted by various stake holders as indicated above. There is an urgent need for India to adopt a far more proactive regional approach that seeks to harmonise the responses of Russia, Iran and Central Asian states towards the vital state of Afghanistan. Here are two clear and distinct scenarios pre and post US/NATO withdrawal:

- Prior to any US withdrawal India will perforce have to confine itself to capacity building of the nascent Afghan state, in particular its economy and Armed Forces.
- However, should a US withdrawal/major scaling down of ground forces takes place, the scenario will stand dramatically altered. India may then well have to contemplate more proactive responses to prevent a Pakistan assisted takeover by the Taliban in Kabul. To generate viable response options, India will need to establish a strong congruence with Iran, Russia and the Central Asian states. It would be in India's interest to orchestrate a regional response to the threat of jehadi fundamentalism radiating outwards from a Talibanised Afghanistan. This could lead to the domino effect in Pakistan itself as well as the fragile states of Central Asia. It could seriously affect India's security in Jammu and Kashmir, as well as enhance the terrorist threat profile in Indian cities and economic centres. It

would therefore be prudent for India to build these bridges now with Iran and the Central Asian states. Iran in specific, would be vital for routing any Indian assistance/support to Afghanistan, military, quasi-military, or economic.

REFERENCES

1. Foreign Policy Address at the Council on Foreign Relations. Hillary Rodham Clinton. July 15, 2009. Available at http://www.state.gov/secretary/rm/2009a/july/126071.htm Accessed on 17 July 2009.
2. What's New in the Strategy for Afghanistan and Pakistan. Available at http://www.whitehouse.gov/the_press_office/Whats-New-in-the-Strategy-for-Afghanistan-and-Pakistan/. Accessed on 15 April 2009.
3. Bronwen Roberts. New NATO chief makes maiden visit to Afghanistan. Available at http://www.google.com/hostednews/afp/article/ ALeqM5hVLlnE5IlIIgvuKP5BGclerTd3RQ. Accessed on 08 August 2009.
4. Akbar Borisov. Presidents meet for security summit in Tajikistan. Available at http://www.google.com/hostednews/afp/article/ALeqM5gh_XDpVKqq4oNRYUihbPgnJHNT8g. Accessed on 10 August 2009.
5. Dan Martin. China issues security alert after Al-Qaeda threat. Available at http://www.google.com/hostednews/afp/article/ALeqM5iRNNcnRM_TKZxGC6lABx7z7ZdQgg. on 10 August 2009.
6. Aynak Copper Project is Inaugurated in a Glorious Ceremony. Available at http://mom.gov.af/index.php?page_id=87. Accessed on 10 August 2009.
7. Brigadier Feroz Hassan Khan. Rough Neighbors: Afghanistan and Pakistan. Strategic Insights, Volume II, Issue 1 (January 2003). Available at http://www.ccc.nps.navy.mil/si/jan03/southAsia.asp. Accessed on 10 August 2009.
8. *Ibid.*
9. Maria Golovnina. Russia wants anti-terror hub in C.Asia -Kyrgyz leader. Available at http://www.reuters.com/article/featuredCrisis/idUSLK594842. Accessed on 10 August 2009.
10. Suman Guha Mozumder. 'India has a constructive role in Afghanistan' Available at http://www.rediff.com/news/2008/jan/31inter.htm. Accessed on 10 August 2009.
11. Visit of Foreign Minister Dr. Rangin Dadfar Spanta of Afghanistan. 28/07/2009. Available at http://meaindia.nic.in/Accessed on 30 July 2009.

6

Alternative Futures: Afghanistan

ALTERNATIVE FUTURES: DEVELOPING EXPLORATORY SCENARIOS

Heuristic forecasting for the purpose of National security can be done scientifically by an in depth study that leads to pattern recognition in the mass of data collated. Since patterns tend to persist and repeat themselves, these constitute useful tools for prognostication and help us to develop insights. There is a need to study the trends and then define the trajectories of events by extrapolating these trends. This helps us to anticipate the future and develop scenarios. For the purposes of developing credible heuristic forecasts these are being developed as Exploratory (rather than Normative Scenarios). This would lead to outlining the plausible/possible Futures that are value neutral (not wished for/ states to be feared/avoided).

Three sets of Alternative futures could be outlined for Afghanistan:-

- Alternative Military Futures
- Alternative Political Futures
- Alternative Economic Futures

The key or *Scenario Defining Driver in the case of Afghanistan would be the outcome of the US/NATO Counter Insurgency campaign in Afghanistan* – in specific, the likely impact of the surge and the overall strategy outlined in the Af-Pak Plan spelt out by President Obama in Mar 09. The outcome in Afghanistan would equally be dependent upon the success or otherwise, of the Pakistani Army's offensive in Swat and FATA. The military trends in Afghanistan have been recounted in detail in the Notes on methodology and again in Chapter Three. These present a dismal scenario because *the COIN campaign in Afghanistan has been seriously under - funded and under - resourced for years.* The easy victory over the Taliban in 2001 was due to the major blunder of the Taliban in fighting set piece battles like a regular Army rather than a guerrilla force using the tactics of dispersal. This easy victory in Op Enduring Freedom generated a high level of hubris in the Pentagon and resulted *in a very small and inadequate footprint of US forces in Afghanistan.* Resources were diverted to Iraq and the Afghan campaign was seriously constrained by a glaring lack of force levels and funding. It is this which enabled the Taliban-Al Qaida combine to regain the initiative and this insurgency has steadily gained in strength from 2005 onwards. The Al Qaida and Taliban were able to get sanctuaries in FATA and NWFP All combat parameters so far make for dismal reading simply because the US and NATO have failed to put adequate boots on the ground. The size of the ANA and Afghan Police has been pegged at 134,000 and 82,000 respectively in the Af-Pak plan. These force levels are far too inadequate to operate in a stand -alone mode post a US withdrawal. This new ANA is primarily a straight legged Infantry force sans armour, artillery or air power. Given the rugged terrain, the force to space ratio and the ratio between the Security Forces and Insurgents, the proposed ANA is far too weak to be able to hold its own in a post US withdrawal scenario. How this 134,000 strong ANA will perform in a post US withdrawal scenario would therefore be a key determinant that will shape future events in Afghanistan. If that is accepted, this force unfortunately is very weak and can only lead to very pessimistic outcomes. Following data is pertinent.

- The *Pre Soviet era Afghan Army was 350,000 strong.* It had 12 Infantry Divisions and three Tank and Three Commando Brigades.
- The *Soviets recreated a viable Afghan Army of five corps that was 550,000 strong* and well equipped on the pattern of Soviet Motorized Rifle Divisions. This force had succeeded in keeping the Mujahideen at bay for over three years after the Soviet withdrawal. It collapsed only because the Soviets pulled out the economic plug.
- If a foot Infantry predominant Afghan Army is envisaged, the Canadians estimate force requirement of nearly 800,000 troops for a viable Army. It is imperative that the ANA be recreated and right sized in a manner that can enable it to take on the bulk of the fighting from the US/NATO forces. This was primarily the Soviet strategy in Afghanistan. They had put in place a minimal

deployment of 120,000 mechanized forces backed by heavy fire power and air support. This force focused upon securing the key cities and road infrastructure in Afghanistan. The Soviets rapidly rebuilt the Afghan Army and pushed it to take on a primary role in the counter guerilla campaign. Military analysts like Anthony Cordesman and SG Jones have advised the US Army to increasingly nativise the conflict by *rapid capacity building of the ANA and enabling it to take on the bulk of the combat.*

The 134,000 strong ANA however, is evidently too small to take on the Taliban in a stand alone mode , or even in a supportive role for long in the "Clear, Hold, Build" format where most of the it will be required to hold territory cleared by the US/ISAF forces. The primary future scenarios in Afghanistan would therefore be a function of the insufficiency of the envisaged ANA in the event of an American withdrawal. It is likely to crumble at best within a year or two of any American/NATO withdrawal of forces.

Success of the Surge: The American Af-Pak plan is trying to replicate the success of the Iraqi troop surge in Afghanistan. A troop surge of 17,000 combat troops and 4000 military trainers is envisaged. How much of an impact this will make will determine the immediate Military Futures in Afghanistan. Will it be a case of too little too late? It will also be dependent upon the degree of success attained by the Pakistani Army in eliminating Taliban sanctuaries in NWFP and FATA. The Alternative Political and Economic Futures would flow out from the Military Futures in Afghanistan. The key determination would be the degree of success that could be achieved by the US Surge in Afghanistan. A key determinant is also *the US will to stay the course in Afghanistan.* The NATO countries are already showing a visible erosion of the political will to stay on and incur more casualties.

ALTERNATIVE MILITARY FUTURES

Any military campaign can have three possible outcomes or end states-it could succeed brilliantly, it could be a moderate or a partial success, or it could prove to be a complete failure. Accordingly the Alternative Military Futures in Afghanistan are three. These are given in the form of a broad flow diagram in the figure below. Key time horizons are the US

Presidential elections (the run up for which commences in 2011) and the estimated time frame in which the proposed ANA may encounter difficulties in managing the campaign against the Taliban after an American withdrawal/draw down of forces. The Three Alternative Military Futures therefore are enumerated below:

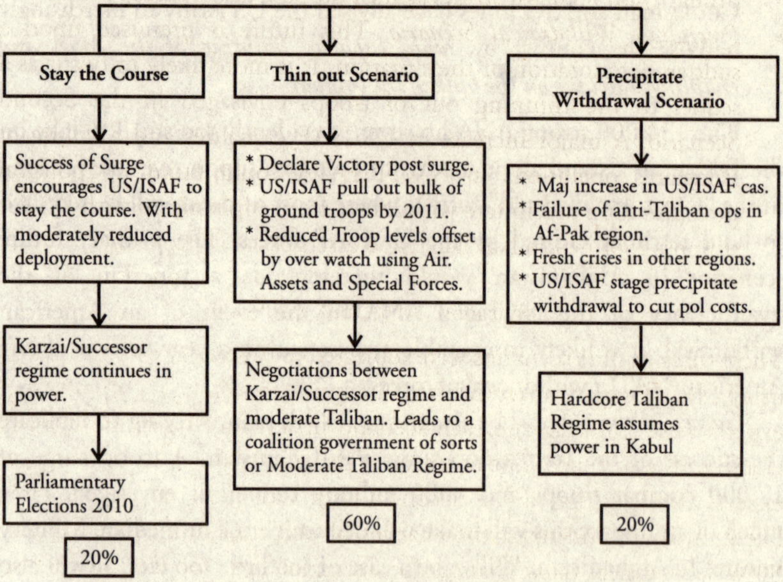

- *Stay the Course Scenario:* This optimistic scenario is premised upon a success of the US surge in Afghanistan. This could have two outcomes either encourage the US and its allies to stay the course (for at least a decade to stabilize the situation) or go in for a thin out of troops. This scenario is predicated upon a degree of military success which encourages the US to stay the course with marginally enhanced/reduced troop commitments to stabilize the situation in Afghanistan on a long term basis through the process of "armed nation state building." This implies that Lt Gen Stanley McChrystal's recommendations of a further troop surge of 40-60,000 is accepted and the size of the ANA and Afghan Police is rapidly doubled.
- *Thin Out Scenario:* This could result from a partial success of the troop surge. This could entail rising casualties for US/NATO troops, the political costs of which may not be acceptable. In view of the forthcoming Presidential elections, President Obama could declare

victory and commence a drawdown of force levels in Afghanistan around 2011. Reduced troop levels on the ground would be offset by over watch using American Air assets and Special Forces in situ. Such a scenario could actualize in a much faster timeframe if Vice President Joe Biden's plan to cut US Ground troops and focus primarily on Predator strikes against the Al Qaeda is accepted.

- *Precipitate Withdrawal Scenario:* This future is premised upon a sudden deterioration of the situation. It is more likely to occur as a sequel to the thinning out of troops envisaged in the Second Scenario. A major increase in US/ISAF casualties and a failure of Pakistan's operations in NWFP/FATA could build up political pressures for a precipitate withdrawal from Afghanistan with US Air support confined to Naval aviation assets based in the Gulf .

CROSS IMPACT MATRIX ANALYSIS

These three outline scenarios were subjected to expert analysis and review using the "Cross Impact Matrix Analysis" technique. The panel of experts were asked to rate each scenario in terms of its credibility and chances of occurrence. The outcome of this analysis is given below. Most experts (less one) rated the Second (Thin Out Scenario) as the most likely outcome and rated the chances of occurrence as between 60 to 80%. One expert rated chances for Scenario One (Stay the Course) as 60%. Chances for this scenario were rated between 10 to 20% by all the other experts. Scenario Three (Precipitate Withdrawal) was rated fairly low by all the experts and quantitative values assigned ranged between 0 to 20 %. Specific expert judgements and their overall average scores for each scenario are summarized in the chart below.

Expert Judgment	Stay the Course I	Thin Out II	Precipitate Withdrawal III
Lt Gen H S Lidder	15%	80%	5%
Lt Gen R Sawhney	20%	70%	10%
Amb G Parthasarthy	20%	70%	10%
Amb R Sikri	25%	75%	0%
Amb Yogendra Kumar	30%	40%	30%
Brig Gurmeet Kanwal	60%	20%	20%
Average	28.33%	59.17%	12.50%

The three scenarios will now be outlined in detail along with an analysis of likely Impact on India.

SCENARIO ONE: STAY THE COURSE

This is an optimistic scenario that is premised upon a significant success of the US Surge in Afghanistan and a concomitant success of the Pakistani operations in NWFP and FATA. It is also premised upon the level of casualties remaining low/within sustainable limits for the USA and its NATO allies.

In such a scenario the Afghan Presidential elections would be relatively smoothly conducted and Hamid Karzai reelected for another five years term in 2009. The Parliamentary and Provincial Elections are equally successfully conducted in 2010.

Encouraged the US decides to stay the course and consolidate the turnaround in Afghanistan. A conscious decision is taken to

- Sustain existing troop levels in Afghanistan.
- Stay the course for 10 years at least.
- It is noteworthy that US troop accommodation being constructed at the Afghan Bases is fairly elaborate and designed for a long stay.
- The US had spent $ 684 Billion in Iraq. However a clear time line for withdrawal has been spelt out from Iraq. So far the US has spent $ 223 Billion on the war in Afghanistan but there is no time line for withdrawal articulated.
- Lt Gen Stanley Mc Chrystal's analysis in Aug 09 asked for 40-60,000 additional troops and a doubling of the ANA and the Afghan Police.
- Afghan Central Govt revenue is US$ 890 mn per year. The ANA and Police budget alone amounts to $ 2 Billion per year.
- Michael. O. Hanlon estimates that for the next 20 years the US will have to provide nearly half the budget for the Afghan Government.
- US could spend up to $ 100 billion a year to continue fighting for a decade in Afghanistan. Up to US $ 4 billion per year will have to be given as military aid and a similar amount as economic assistance each year to Afghanistan.

- The US, feels Hanlen, is creating a long term military aid situation similar to the one with Israel, Egypt or Jordan.
- Stephen Biddle has stated that US will need a long combat presence for many years to come and a financial commitment for an even longer duration. Assistant Secretary for Defense B West has wondered if the Congress will support such long term funding.
- The US is likely to stay engaged in Afghanistan at least till 2020 at the current/slightly enhanced force levels. This constitutes the Stay the Course Scenario.

IMPACT ON INDIA

This is the best scenario as it serves Indian interests at the lowest costs. This implies a continuation of the status quo.

- It would be in India's interests to encourage the US/ISAF to stay the course in Afghanistan.
- India should continue/intensify its economic aid to Afghanistan.
- Invest in Infrastructure creation.
- Build schools/hospitals. Invest heavily in Educational sector, especially IT.
- Assist in mineral extraction in Northern Provinces where conditions are relatively stable. Develop Iron, Copper and Gold mining facilities.
- Build Power stations.
- Provide Telephone, mobile and Internet connectivity.
- Support high value agriculture.
- Restore canal (Karez system) for Irrigation. Promote drip irrigation.
- Set up Veterinary hospitals and Dairy Projects.
- Encourage Cotton production and establish cloth mills.
- Set up Solar and Wind farms for power generation.

QUASI MILITARY

- India should avoid any committal of troops while the American/ISAF present.

- However, as part of capacity building, India could offer to finance, equip and train one/two divisions of the ANA.
- India could also offer to provide equipment and training for two/three Armoured Regiments. (Old Soviet era T-54/T-55 Tanks could be supplied) as also up to three Regiments of Artillery (with ammunition) to enable capacity building of the Afghan Armed forces.
- Continue to train Afghan Military, Police and Civilian officials in Indian training institutions.

SCENARIO TWO: THIN OUT SCENARIO

- The anchor premise of this scenario is the political compulsion of US/ISAF countries to cut political costs of mounting casualties. ISAF countries like Canada, Netherlands, Germany and France may pull out troops by 2012 due to the rising political cost of casualties. This in turn could put tremendous pressure on America to withdraw/thin out its troops.
- Since US Presidential Elections are due in 2012, President Obama could declare the surge successful and order pull out of troops from Afghanistan in 2011 (when the Presidential re election campaign starts off). This Thin Out scenario could however occur in 2010 itself if Vice President Joe Biden's plan is accepted.
- A bulk of the American ground troops would be withdrawn in a phased manner. However these reduced troop levels would be offset by basing air assets at major air bases like Bagram and Kandhar etc along with Special Forces Contingents.
- President Karzai would be compelled to hold negotiations with the moderate Taliban and come to a negotiated settlement that enforces temporary ceasefires and peace talks to accommodate these element in the government. A coalition government may well emerge with Talibani elements.
- Bulk of US/ISAF forces would withdraw by 2012 and thereby cut the political costs of the casualties being incurred in this campaign.
- Given the inadequate size and equipment pattern of the ANA, the

situation could rapidly deteriorate within a year of the US/ISAF withdrawal.

- US Air Bases/SF Force bases could specifically be targeted by Taliban suicide bombers and rocket/IED attacks to cause casualties and raise political costs that could force them to withdraw.
- The prime danger in this scenario is the high risk of a rapid deterioration to scenario three(Precipitate Withdrawal)
- This could occur if the ISI decides to intervene (as it had in the earlier Taliban campaign of the 1990s). It had then inducted some 11-12,000 Pakistani troops of Pashtun extraction (in mufti) who manned the Taliban's tanks, artillery and heavy weapons and enabled it to fight like a regular army. Pakistani pilots had also flown the Soviet era Jets of the Taliban.
- Over a period of two to three years, this may encourage the Taliban to switch to regular operations to complete the military subjugation of the whole of Afghanistan. Saudi Arabia could well provide finances to buy off the opposition (as it had in the 1990s).

IMPACT ON INDIA

- The Afghan nation state had been comprehensively destroyed by the covert war of the CIA/Saudi Arabia/ISI. So far the USA has contributed some US$ 32 billion for raising/equipping the ANA/Police and providing economic aid for reconstruction. The other nation like Japan, EU countries, Canada, China, India etc. have contributed a total of some US$50 billion. Keeping in view the very limited revenue base of the Afghan State ($890 million per year) Afghanistan will need up to US$ 8 billion aid per year for the next one to two decades (4 billion for the ANA/Police and 4 billion for civilian economic aid and reconstruction).
- India is not in position to take on such a huge financial burden by itself. It could at best provide aid worth a billion dollars per year.
- *Regional Approach:* It would therefore be very much in India's interests to try and create a regional consensus/coalition of like- minded states (in specific Iran, Central Asia, Russia and co-opt Japan) to sustain the Afghan nation state with economic and military aid.

- *Military Intervention:* Should the situation deteriorate badly in Afghanistan, India could receive requests for military aid from the Afghan Govt in Kabul (especially if the ISI inducts Pashtun troops to enable the Taliban to switch to regular warfare). India will need to do military capacity building now to be able to respond to such requests (when and if these are made).
- *Regional Coalition/Un Mission:* However India (if at all) must take care to get involved militarily only as part of a Regional Coalition/ a UN Mission under Chapter Seven (or six and a half as here to fore)
- *Logistical Support via Iran:* Currently no appreciable force can be committed to Afghanistan for lack of a logistical support capability. It would be essential for India to generate this logistical capacity via Iran .
- Supplies could be routed via the Sea to the ports of Chah Bahar and Bandar Abbass in Iran. To that extent Iranian support would be vital.
- India therefore needs to invest now in developing the road axis from Chabahar to Zahedan and on onwards to Zaranj and Dilaram on the Afghan ring Road. The major reliance may have to be placed on the Bandar Abbas route as the route from Chabahar is infested with Baluch insurgents hostile to the Iranian regime.
- This passes through the disturbed territory of Iranian Baluchistan and is fairly close to the Pakistani border. It could be interfered with by the Jandollah/Taliban in its Afghan section (Dilaram to Zaranj).
- Alternative supply lines from Bandar Abbas to Herat would have to be relied upon primarily in case there is a need to logistically sustain forces in Afghanistan.
- *Capacity Building of ANA:* However India's preferred option should be the capacity building of the ANA to be able to fight the Taliban. Towards this end India could offer to pay for, raise. equip and train up to
- 2x Afghan Infantry Division
- 1x Armoured Brigade (T-54/T-55 tanks)
- 1x Artillery Brigade (75/ 24mm/ 25 Pounders).
- India would need to work in close concert with Iran to prevent the re emergence of a Taliban regime in Iran.

- *Indirect Military Pressure:* Till such time as strong and viable logistical options are developed via Iran, India's sole military response options could be to put pressure on Pakistan's Eastern borders to reduce its capacity for interference in Afghanistan.
- *Air Bases:* To create capacities for supporting the beleaguered Afghan regime in Kabul India could explore the option of securing Air base facilities in Iran, Tajikistan or Uzbekistan to be able to provide Air support in an emergency situation.

SCENARIO THREE: PRECIPITATE WITHDRAWAL

- This scenario could actualize if US and ISAF troops suffer inordinately high casualties in the Surge operations.
- A precipitate withdrawal would logically follow within one/two or more years after a Thin Out Scenario (by 2014-2015).
- The US Air/SF Bases in Afghanistan could be the targets of Taliban suicide bombers IED's or even Rocket attacks to force the remaining US Troops to withdraw.
- The ISI could up the ante by providing Pashtun soldiers from the Pak Army and heavy weapons support (in the 1990s it had provided tanks, artillery and fighter support to the Taliban). This could enable the Taliban to switch back to regular/large scale operations after the US withdrawal. A strengthened Taliban could then launch a military offensive to seize the major cities (Kandahar, Jalalabad, Herat and Kabul). This may lead to a revival of the Northern Alliance and may result in a defacto partition of Afghanistan along ethnic fault lines. The Taliban had carried out ethnic cleansing campaigns in the 1990s against the Hazaras and Uzbeks and sharply polarized the ethnic divisions in Afghanistan. A Taliban regime in Kabul could well lead to a partition of that country along ethnic Pashtun-Farsiwan fault lines.
- The Talibanisation of Afghanistan however could have a major blow back effect on Pakistan itself. It could lead to a rise of fundamentalist elements in the Army and ISI itself.
- Should Taliban influence in Pakistan spread West of the Indus, it

could pose credible security threat to the safety of Pakistan nuclear arsenal.

- Serious unrest/instability in Pakistan could generate large scale refugee problem in India's Western borders.

IMPACT ON INDIA

- This could be the worst case scenario for India and would pose a serious threat to its Security.
- A fundamentalist, hard core Taliban regime in Kabul (even the Hekmatyar/Haqquani factions) would have a very adverse impact on Indian Security.
- India and Iran may have no option thereafter but to revive and support the Northern Alliance and any elements opposed to the Taliban in Afghanistan.
- India should examine the feasibility of an Op Jupiter type operation to rescue the Karzai/successor regime in such a worst case scenario.
- India may well have to put military pressure on Pakistan's Eastern Front to force it to call off/scale down its support to the Taliban.

LONG TERM STRATEGIC FUTURES: PROBABLE SCENARIOS

All long term futures that span a time horizon of 10-15 years would be a logical outgrowth of what happens in the near term future, i.e. the success or otherwise of the US surge. Results of this would be evident by 2011-2012. Based upon these probable end states/outcomes, a range of long term future probabilities can be outlined. These however would be purely hypothetical scenarios based upon probability. These hypothetical end states can be listed as follows:

- Stabilisation of a Nation State in Afghanistan
- Fragmentation along Ethnic Fault Lines. This could take two forms:-
    * Taliban's Pashtun Consolidation.
    * Emergence of Pakhtun Khwa that leads to a splintering of Pakistan.

These long term futures merit elaboration.

Stabilisation of a Nation State in Afghanistan: The long term success of armed nation state building could lead to the positive outcome of the stabilisation of a relatively modernist and inclusive state in Afghanistan that is self-sustaining and resists external penetration/control.

Fragmentation along Ethnic Faultlines: The Taliban had practiced politics of ethnic exclusion and even the ethnic cleansing of Hazara and Uzbek minorities from the 1990s to 2001. This has deepened ethnic polarisation in Afghanistan. A Taliban resurgence in Afghanistan is likely to lead to the fragmentation of that state along ethnic faultlines. Such fragmentation could assume two forms:

- *Taliban's Pashtun Consolidation:* The ISI has consciously tried to *subsume Afghan nationalism by promoting the Salafi ideology of Jihad via the Taliban,* to make national frontiers irrelevant. It has been its constant endeavour to gain strategic depth in Afghanistan. The Taliban insurgency has made the Durand Line irrelevant. If the Taliban insurgency triumphs, Pakistan could gain control of the Pashtun areas of Afghanistan and expand territorially to gain the notional strategic depth.
- *Emergence of Pashtun Khwa:* However, given the degree of alienation that could be caused by the Pakistan Army operations in NWFP and FATA, the reverse could equally happen. A new Pashtun national entity that straddles the Durand Line could come into being. If Afghanistan survives, its capital would remain in Kabul. Should Afghanistan fragment on ethnic Faultlines, the new Pakhtun Khwa could emerge as a result of the splintering of Pakistan along the Indus Faultline. The new entity may seek its capital in Peshawar. The Pashtuns therefore could create a state at the expense of Pakistan.

Fate of Baluchistan: In the long term strategic calculus, the fate of Baluchistan would become even more critical than the ultimate outcome in Afghanistan. This would be simply because the geo-political stakes involved in Baluchistan are far higher than those involved in Afghanistan. Baluchistan dominates the Persian Gulf coast line. The Baluch ethnic area has two significant ports in Gwadar and Chahbahar (in Iran). Gwadar plays a critical role in the Chinese Grand Strategy to bypass the key choke point of the Mallacca Straits, (which is China's most significant vulnerability in terms of its energy security). It gives the Chinese Navy a key port dominating the critical Persian Gulf waterway. The USA would not bc keen to see this happen and is likely to covertly/overtly contest such attempts by the Chinese to gain influence and control over this key coast line. Baluchistan is rich in energy resources and strategic minerals and is bound to become a zone of very keen strategic contention between regional and extra- regional powers.

IMPACT ON INDIA

- From the Indian security point of view, the best case scenario is the stabilisation of the current relatively modernist state in Afghanistan (albeit in a more ethnically inclusive form).
- The worst case scenario would be a takeover of the whole or the Pashtun parts of Afghanistan by the hardcore Taliban-Al Qaida combine. It could pose a serious threat to Indian and regional security.
- Emergence of a Pakhtun Khwa that straddles the Durand Line could lead to the splintering of Pakistan with unpredictable consequences for regional and global security. The prime global concern then would be the safety of Pakistan's nuclear arsenal.

AFGHANISTAN: ALTERNATIVE POLITICAL FUTURES

Constitutional Loya Jirga (CLJ)

A country's Constitutional Assembly debates provide a vital insight into the primary issues that animate its political discourse. There were heated debates in the Constitutional Loya Jirga (CLJ) in end 2003 and beginning 2004. In fact in Jan 2004, the debate reached a dead lock with 40% of the delegates staying away. The deadlock was largely on ethnic fault-lines and the three key issues of discourse were:

- Power of the Presidency The Pashtuns favoured a highly centralised state with a strong Presidency. The Tajiks, Uzbeks and Hazaras were in favour of a Federal Parliamentary democracy. The Tajiks ultimately agreed to a Presidential system as the basis of power sharing.

- *Lack of Effective Powers for Provincial Legislatures:* A multi ethnic society like Afghanistan needs Federalism. However fears of state collapse have impelled the Afghans to go in for a highly centralised state. The fiscal and administrative powers of the Provincial legislatures are very limited and the Governors are not elected but appointed by the Centre. Once again the views were split on ethnic fault lines.
- *Lack of Language Rights:* Pashto was proposed to be the only national language and not Dari. The Tajiks, Hazaras and Uzbeks demanded language rights, which were opposed by the Pashtuns. Finally after heated debate provincial languages were recognised. This could promote dual identities and "language communities" in Afghanistan.

SALIENT CHARACTERISTICS OF THE AFGHAN POLITICAL SCENE

- The current political dispensation in Afghanistan was shaped in the aftermath of the runaway success of Op Enduring Freedom. It was influenced by the high levels of hubris prevalent at that time. As per American wishes, Afghanistan has gone for a highly Centralized State and a Presidential System that *is currently very dependent on a charismatic and strong leader like President Hamid Karzai who has a pan- Afghan acceptance.*
- The Americans had strongly influenced the choice towards the Presidential system (possibly as an antidote to the rampant war-lordism then rife in Afghanistan). US Ambassador Zalmay Khalilzad and the UN special Representative Lakhdhar Brahimi, had strongly influenced the outcome of the CLJ debates.
- In President Karzai, Afghanistan presently has a charismatic Pashtun politician with a pan-Afghan stature. However this makes the working of the present system overly dependent on some key personalities and individuals. It has yet not thrown up strong institutions that could manage ethnic tensions on a long term basis.
- *In theory, the Karzai dispensation is a strongly centralised state (some feel over centralised). However in practice, the current Afghan Government's*

writ hardly runs outside Kabul (President Karzai is often referred to as the Mayor of Kabul). This glaring gap between theory and practice is significant and will need to be closely watched.

THE MULTI-ETHNIC CHARACTER OF THE AFGHAN STATE

- The CIA estimates the current population of Afghanistan at 33 million (2008). The Central Statistics Institute of Afghanistan put it at 22 million in 2002. The Afghan census was postponed to beyond 2010 as it is likely to be controversial. The current demographic break up is broadly as under:
  Pashtuns - 42%
  Tajiks - 27%
  Uzbeks - 9 %
  Hazaras - 9%
  Others - 13%
- The Pashtuns, though the largest single ethnic group do not constitute a majority. Besides they are divided on tribal lines. Other estimates of the Pashtuns peg it as low as 38%and the Tajiks as high as 37%.
- *Taliban's Polarisation of Ethnic Identities:* The Taliban tried to forcefully reassert the traditional Pashtun domination in Afghanistan. Its strongly ethnic exclusionary politics had served to sharply polarize Afghan society along ethnic fault lines (primarily Pashtun vs Farsiwan identities). In fact, in 1997-8, the Taliban carried out ethnic cleansing of the Shia Hazaras that almost led to a war with Iran. It later carried out ethnic cleansing in Mazar-e-Sharief and invited a retaliatory bloodbath. To that extent a Taliban regime in Kabul could lead to a partition of the country along ethnic fault lines and must therefore be avoided. The fact of recent history that must be highlighted is the sharp polarisation of Afghan society along ethnic fault-lines that had been generated by the blatantly exclusionary ethnic politics of the Taliban from 1995-2001.
- Perception of past treatment, writes Katherine Adeney in her highly perceptive paper (Constitutional Design and the Political Salience of

Community Identity in Afghanistan), demonstrated why preferences determined by ethnicity were at the heart of the constitutional debates in the CLJ in Afghanistan.

- She highlights that any perception of ethnically dominated centre discriminating against territorially concentrated ethnic Groups (especially Uzbek and Hazara) will invariably lead to major disaffection and potential tensions.
- The Presidential System represents a Zero Sum Game in that there can be only one winner from one community (Lijphant).
- Katherine Adeney writes that "Centralization without power sharing at the Center in ethnically divided societies has the potential to alienate ethnic communities, especially if they are territorially concentrated. In this respect the Uzbek and Hazara communities now are feeling alienated and unless managed this could lead to ethnic separatism/insurgencies.
- Katherine writes that if "if Provincial Councils are unable to be effective institutions of government, an ethnic backlash could further undermine the sense of national identity. The Afghanistan Research and Evaluation Unit states that though Provincial Councils are mandated to contribute to planning but they are not administrative and fiscal structures which can make provincial autonomy functional.
- *Absence of Political Parties:* This will be compounded if the center becomes paralysed in the absence of national parties. The absence of strong political parties will not work in favour of political unity and may well lead to instability in parliament. After the experience of Khalq and Parcham parties, there is a strong antipathy amongst the Afghan elite for political parties.
- *Quotas and Meritocracy:* The Afghan constitution (Article 50) opts for recruitment on the basis of ability/merit and rules out ethnic quotas. Merit based appointments however tend to reinforce historical ethnic domination through rewarding past privilege. Merit based appoints, feels Katherine, will only prevent tension amongst communities if these are perceived as fair and generally representative of society. An unconscious quota system has seeped in

and Karzai's cabinet is ethnically fairly balanced (Even though three key ministries - Defence, Interior and Finance are with Pashtuns). The current cabinet ethnics is as under:

Pashtun - 10
Tajik - 08
Hazara - 05
Uzbek - 02
Turkoman - 01
Baloch - 01

- *Two Vice Presidents:* The CLJ insisted upon two Vice Presidents. These are currently from the Tajik and Hazara communities. Katherine writes that for future stability, the two Vice Presidents will have to be more than symbolic, but be powerful leaders in their own communities. This two Vice President system does not create a balance in the political dispensation and overtime could throw up a corpus of pan-Afghan leaders.
- Katherine writes, "Despite President Karzai's ability to secure support from all communities in the Presidential Election of 2004, he is only one man and an increasingly vulnerable one at that. The current dispensation therefore is far too dependent upon individual personalities that have a pan-Afghan acceptability. The existing constitutional provisions appear to be a sensible compromise in a fluid, post conflict situation, they are too *dependent on only one individual, President Hamid Karzai, for their constitutional success.*
- *Discredited Warlords:* In their haste to reestablish a nation state destroyed by three decades of war, the current Karzai dispensation had little choice but to cooperate with the existing power centres. These warlords were notoriously corrupt and high handed and their initial depredations in the post Soviet scenario had led to the rise of the Taliban. The reliance upon these same discredited warlords needlessly sullied the image of the Karzai regime and undercut the concept of merit and ability. The corrupt practices of these former warlords have largely been responsible for alienating the population from the Karzai government and giving a fillip to the Taliban insurgency. Had the US invested in rapidly creating an Afghan

National Army, reliance upon the warlords could been greatly reduced and a nation state stabilized. A key result area therefore would be the rapid creation of an Afghan ANA and bureaucracy based upon merit and a greater degree of federalism that gives more fiscal and administrative power to the provincial legislatures. The current system is far too over centralised and brittle and not likely to last long.

AFGHANISTAN: ALTERNATIVE POLITICAL FUTURES

- There is a strong sense of national identity in Afghanistan. Even though it is considered a rentier state in economic terms, from 1919 to 1979, Afghanistan existed as a viable and largely self sufficient state. After four decades of war the Afghan people are yearning for peace and stability and there is a strong undercurrent of hope and optimism for the future. Their agricultural economy was destroyed by the huge migration of approximately 33% of the population to Pakistan and Iran. The ignominy of life in refugee camps has strengthened their yearning for nationhood.
- The current over centralised Provincial System is too highly dependent upon a single charismatic personality with a pan-Afghan appeal (President Karzai). The present constitutional arrangements are far too dependent on only one individual for their constitutional success.
- *Wild Card Scenario:* The sudden demise/success of Talibani assassination attempts could create a severe crisis in present day Afghanistan. It suggests a need for foolproof security of the Afghan President. However in the long term, institutions must take primacy over individuals, and Afghanistan will have to take a fresh look at its institutions for managing ethnic diversity in a sustainable manner.
- *Need for Federalism:* David Cameroon has argued that Afghanistan is a perfect candidate for federalism. Its provincial assemblies must therefore be given greater fiscal and administrative powers, and provincial governors must be elected and not appointed by the center.
- Although the current political discourse seems more focused on issues like security, opium production, economic development and

prosecution of war criminals, serious ethnic tensions could easily reassert themselves if these power sharing agreements are not put in place quickly.

- *Ethnic Separatism:* Katherine Adeney writes that, "Ethnic harmony within Afghanistan may be much more precarious than is often assumed."
- *Uzbek and Hazara Alienation:* The dangers of Uzbek and Hazara alienation are most acute and unless managed properly, these could lead to the rise of separatist sentiments in these territorially concentrated communities.
- *Tribal Militias:* In June 2006, the Afghan government formed tribal militias in southern Afghanistan to cater for the insufficient strength of ANA and Police to gaurd these areas. These have led to complaints by the Northern areas that the government is collecting arms from the Northern Militias but giving arms to the South. Alliances made with resurgent Taliban in the South contrast markedly with the government demands that political parties affiliated with the Uzbek Generals Dostam and Abdul Malik be disbanded on the grounds that they continue to maintain military wings. These developments do not augur well for reducing ethnic tensions in Afghanistan. Alienation amongst the constituents of the former Northern Alliance will have to be managed deftly and intelligently.
- *United National Front:* In early 2007 an opposition group called United National Front was formed by former President Burhanuddin Rabbani. This includes Karzai's own Vice President (Tajik Ahmaad Zai Mahsood), Uzbek Dostam and the Tajik Ismail Khan. It has an important ethnic dimension, even though it is trying to give itself a national character by having Pashtun members (grandson of former king, Zahir Shah, is a member). The aim is to seek greater power for provincial assemblies and direct election of governors. This could lead to political polarisation and may bring about a degree of federalism in an over centralised political dispensation which could prove to be too brittle and even dangerous for a multi-ethnic society. The precedent of Sri Lanka is ominous. It is noteworthy that Article 35 of the Afghan constitution prohibits

the formation and operation of a party on the basis for tribalism, parochialism, language as well a religious sectarianism. This is in keeping with the desire of many Afghan political elite to marginalise ethnic identities, but could lead to a lack of mechanisms to sublimate ethnic conflict and deal with issues of identity. The formation of the United National Front could be the precursor for the formation of a party system. It would help if it leads to greater devolution of fiscal and administrative powers to the provinces.

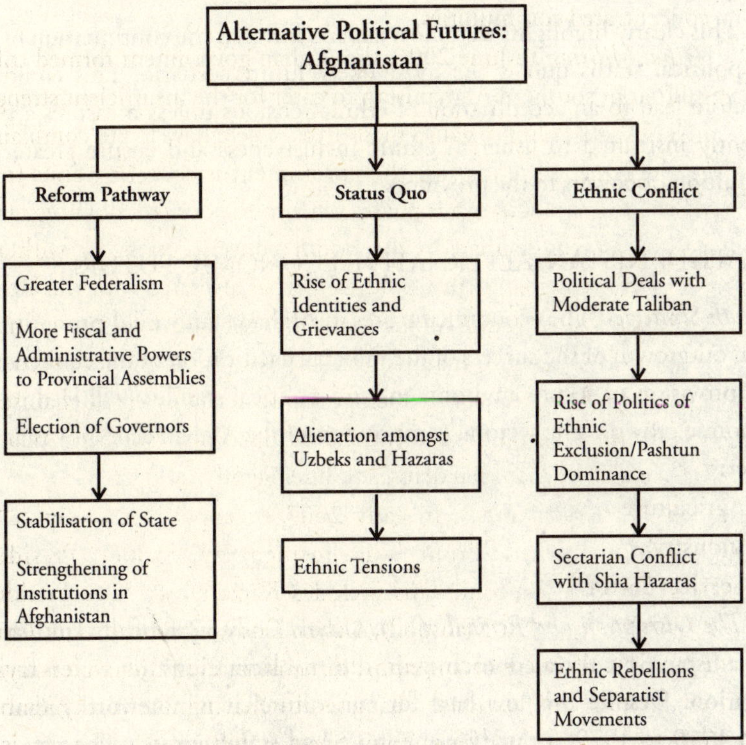

Cross Impact Matrix Analysis

The above matrix of political futures was subjected to a cross impact matrix analysis. The panel of experts was asked to rate the probability of each future actualizing in percentile terms. Their quantified judgment analysis is reproduced below.

Expert	Reform Pathway	Status Quo	Ethnic Exclusion
Lt Gen H S Lidder	15%	60%	35%
Lt Gen R Sawhney	20%	70%	10%
Amb G Parthasarthy	30%	40%	30%
Amb R Sikri	20%	50%	30%
Amb Yogendra Kumar	30%	40%	30%
Brig Gurmeet Kanwal	30%	40%	30%
Average	23.50%	50%	26.50%

This clearly highlights that most experts feel that the continuation of the political status quo is the most likely future scenario. This could therefore lead to an accentuation of ethnic tensions unless measures are urgently instituted to usher in ethnic inclusiveness and ensure greater devolution of powers to the provinces.

AFGHANISTAN: ALTERNATIVE ECONOMIC FUTURES

Growth Strategies: The economic futures in Afghanistan would primarily be an outgrowth of the success of the military pacification of the country. The provision of secure environment and political stability will lead to economic growth. The sectoral composition of the Afghan economy is as under:

- Agriculture
- Industry
- Services Sector

The Disruption and Revival of Agriculture: Only 12% of the land in Afghanistan is cultivated each year due to limitations of water for irrigation. Despite this low base for agriculture, it is noteworthy that from 1919 to 1979, a purely viable state had stabilized in Afghanistan that was self sufficient in terms of food security for its sparse population. Afghanistan was producing sufficient food grains for its needs as also high value agriculture products for export. This agricultural base of its economy has been severely disrupted by four decades of war. The agriculture was manpower intensive. Some 9% of the Afghan population was killed. Some 33% fled and 11% were internally displaced (mostly to urban areas). Major segments of the canal (Karez) system were bombed and large tracts of arable land rendered unusable by large scale mine laying. In such circumstances, opium, a crop that was not labour intensive, became the mainstay of wartime Afghan economy. Afghanistan now needs to import one million tons of wheat annually to support its population. There is a need to revive Afghan agriculture by:

- Rehabilitation the refugees/internally displaced populations to provide the inputs for labour intensive food crops.
- Demine the area on priority.
- Focus on high value agriculture like dry fruits.
- Restore the irrigation system. Promote Drip Irrigation.

Opium: The War Time Economy—Fuel of Terrorism: In a country where close to 50% of the peasant population had been killed, injured or had fled, traditional labour intensive crops were not a feasible proportion. Over time the opium production in the Golden Crescent came to be a major source of finance for the Jihad against the Soviet Union. It is noteworthy that Gulbuddin Hekmatyar's Hizb-e-Islami was closely involved in it. Trucks from the ISI National Logistics Cell would deliver weapons and munitions to Hekmatyar's forces and carry back the opium to Pakistan. Here it was processed into Heroine and smuggled to Europe and USA. When CIA's support to Hekmatyar declined and stopped after the exit of Soviet forces in 1989, Hekmatyar switched almost entirely to drugs to finance his operations inside Afghanistan. This wartime economy has also become the subsistence economy in Afghanistan. Destruction of poppy crops by itself will not suffice to root out the problem.

Lessons from the Golden Triangle: The poor Afghan farmers will have to be given alternate means of livelihood. One of the best examples is Thailand's highly successful attempts to wean its tribes in the Golden Triangle from poppy cultivation. They were given Swiss Government grants and encouraged to grow McDermott (one of the most expensive variants of Almond) for export and also switch to coffee plantation. These alternative means for livelihood cushioned the economic impact of the switch and incentivized the tribal farmers to change to dry fruits that yielded even higher returns to them. It is noteworthy that in 2003,

Afghanistan had a record wheat harvest. When during the draught, the prices of wheat rose, a large number of farmers switched to growing wheat because its cultivation became remunerative. The Afghan traditional labour intensive agriculture will have to be revived, the land demined and irrigation infrastructure rebuilt. Farmers will have to be incentivized to switch to high value agriculture in terms of dry fruits/pomegranates, et al. Prior to the Soviet invasion, 65% of the dry fruits exported worldwide were sourced from Afghanistan. Post 1989, this fell to just16% and must be revived.

Mineral Extraction: Afghanistan is rich in minerals especially copper, iron, gold and precious/semi-precious stones. The Chinese have invested US$ 3 billion in the Aynak copper mines of Logar province. These alone will yield a royalty of US$ 400 million per annum. Estimates of oil reserves in Afghanistan have been revised by the US Geological Survey by a factor of 15 and that of natural gas as a factor of three. Prior to the Soviet invasion Afghanistan was earning US$ 300 million per year from exports of natural gas, which contributed to 56% of the exports. These could be revived and could earn Afghanistan two to three times of the same annually. Most of the mineral resources are in the Northern Provinces which are relatively far more peaceful. To revive a viable and self-sustaining economy in Afghanistan, its mineral wealth must be fully exploited.

Live stock: Afghanistan had some 20 million sheep and 3.3 million goats prior to the invasion. Live stock accounted for 7% of the GDP and to 51% of the exports. This must be revived on priority. These aspects will be taken up in detail in next chapter.

Alternative Economic Failures: Post the fall of Taliban, the USA and other countries of the world have provided some US$ 82 billion worth aid (military and economic) to revive the Afghan state. The intensification of the Taliban insurgency has greatly impeded the economic revival of Afghanistan especially in its Southern provinces. The recurring annual aid required for Afghanistan would be of the order of US$ 8 billion per annum for the next 10 years, at the least. Of this, some US$ 4 billion per annum would be needed as security expenditure on the Afghan Army and Police. The annual revenue of the Afghan Government is just US$ 890 million per year. Copper royalties and natural gas sales could increase it by almost US$ 1 billion per year. Leather and dairy exports could enhance it further. Gold Jewellery and diamonds are a major export product of India. These could develop back linkages with the Gold mines in Northern Afghanistan, as also utilize their precious and semi-precious stones.

The alternative economic futures therefore relate to:

- Continuation of US/Western Aid for one to two decades at the recurring rate of about US$ 8 billion per annum.
- Termination of US/Western Aid within the next four to five years and a need for regional power economies to step in.

Afghanistan is now a member of SAARC and SAFTA, and it would be in India's interests to revive its economy and develop strong linkages with it via train. Pakistan should be encouraged to provide access for trade and commercial links with Afghanistan, if necessary under the pretext of establishing trade links with Nepal, Bhutan and Bangladesh. A long term revival of the Afghan economy would require the development of strong structural linkages with the most vibrant economy in South Asia. Traditionally, India was the market for Afghanistan fruits and high value agricultural products. These traditional linkages with the Indian economy will need to be revived via Iran (and to the extent possible through Pakistan) and reinforced. Indian firms must be encouraged to trade with and invest in Afghanistan. To begin with this, linkages could be developed with the more relatively peaceful Northern provinces.

REFERENCES

1. Anthony H Cordesman, *"US Strategy for Afghanistan: Achieving Peace and Stability in the Graveyard of Empires,"* Centre for Strategic and International Studies (CSIS).
2. Barnett Rubin, "The Way Forward in Afghanistan: Three Views," *Survival: Global Politics & Strategy*, Feb-Mar 2009 issue.
3. Robert Gates cited in "The Way Forward in Afghanistan: Three Views," *Survival: Global Politics & Strategy*, Feb-Mar 2009 issue.
4. Julian Lindley French cited in "The Way Forward in Afghanistan: Three Views," *Survival: Global Politics & Strategy*, Feb-Mar 2009 issue.
5. Antonio Giustozzi "Koran, Kalashnikov and Laptop; The Neo-Taliban Insurgency in Afghanistan," Foundation Books (reprint) New Delhi 2007.

6. Elizabeth Gould And Paul Fitzgerald, *"Invisible History: Afghanistan's Untold Story,"* Brassey and Pergemon, New York 2008.
7. Seth G Jones *"Counter Insurgency in Afghanistan,"* Rand Corporation Study prepared for the Office of the Secretary of Defense. Santa Monica USA, 2008.
8. Katherine Adney "Constitutional Design and the Salience of Political Identity in Afghanistan," *Asian Survey,* Vol. XLVIII No 4, Jul-Aug 2008.

7

Nation State Reconstruction Matrix: Economic Reconstruction and Military Consolidation

INTRODUCTION

'Ra sa warwa da dastan, Nek wa bad pa kse bayan;
Ham abrat ham naishat dai, Pre di poh si danayan.'

(Come hear this tale, Good and bad are shown in it.
It is alike warning and counsel. Wise men, take note of it)

[Khushal Khan Khattak, Pashto poet and anti-government Pathan tribal warrior-leader in the time of the Mughal Emperor Aurangzeb]

The Afghan Government in Kabul as well as the Western powers and their camp-followers who are providing the foreign armed forces in Afghanistan are facing immense problems in establishing the control of the Afghan government over most of the country. The problems being faced have been the subject of much thought and writings in recent years, from about 2002 onwards.

The two related aspects discussed hereafter are those critical to the future stability of Afghanistan:

(1) Economic reconstruction and

(2) The military consolidation that is necessary to ensure that it survives and allows Afghanistan to recover.

The macro-economists at the major international institutions such as the World Bank, the UN's Food and Agriculture Organisation (FAO), and all others, are agreed on the basic course of action needed for the desired economic revival. For the military consolidation needed, however, opinions differ, primarily because of the differing viewpoints and perspectives of those making these judgments. This study will make its own judgment on what is deemed necessary, or what the re-created Afghan National Army (ANA) should be, from the author's own assessment of its political requirements.

ECONOMIC RECONSTRUCTION

An often overlooked fact is that from 1919, to the time of the Soviet invasion and subsequent occupation of Afghanistan from end-December 1979 onwards, Afghanistan has been a self-sufficient state in respect of food and the basic necessities of life. A largely rural society and economy, it had preserved an agro-economic system more or less intact from the medieval era. This served the country well; the overwhelming majority of the people did not go hungry, even though only a very few were rich. The political upheavals of the last three decades have completely shattered this system. The task, therefore, is to revive or re-create the same system as far as possible.

The key factors that will allow the economic system to revive are:

- Physical security for the inhabitants, which can only follow from political stability and the state's ability to enforce the safety and well-being of everyone. The military part of this requirement will be discussed in the next section.
- Revival of agriculture to 1979 levels of productivity, as a pre-requisite to further growth and improvement. This in itself has two immediate requirements: (1) de-mining of agricultural lands, and (2) restoration of the 1979 water management system, with further improvements as a follow-on.
- Resumption of local and international trade, restoration of the traditional trading practices, and a subsequent incremental development of modern financial systems, including Islamic banking practices.
- Collection of taxes from the provinces by the Afghan government.
- Restoration of the education system, and a simultaneous creation of jobs for the youth.

REVIVAL OF AGRICULTURE

Afghanistan has considerable agricultural potential, even though only 12 per cent of the land is arable. This potential is realizable, provided that the water management system of the country, for irrigation in particular, is brought to a state where it is first restored to 1979 levels and then greatly improved. Prior to the Soviet invasion, 85 per cent of the country's population lived in the rural areas, and were rural subsistence farmers entirely dependent upon agriculture. Agriculture accounted for roughly 85 per cent of the country's GDP. Today, what agriculture is left is either subsistence agriculture, or a profitable monoculture of opium poppy cultivation.

Between 1980 and 2001, between 53% and 67% of all villages had been bombed; 24% to 36% of the country's irrigation systems had been destroyed; and the number of livestock had fallen by 70%. By 1987, thirty percent of the country's irrigation system had been destroyed, primarily through intentional bombing or mining. Fertilizer use had declined by ninety percent. By 1989, the agricultural community had declined from 85% to 23% of the population. There has been no significant improvement in these figures.

These changes have completely altered the former agricultural economy of Afghanistan. It has affected both those crops which made the country self-sufficient in food, and the cash crops, which includes the crops that were produced for export. It will suffice for the purposes of this study to briefly examine only a few of the major significant crops.

Wheat: Though Afghanistan grew a number of cereal crops, including maize, barley, and even rice, wheat was the single most important cereal crop. Its importance can be judged from the fact that wheat formed roughly 80 per cent of the average Afghan's dietary intake. In the decade 1980-1990, wheat production declined by 30 per cent, and has declined further since. Afghanistan grows both varieties of bread wheat, winter wheat and summer wheat, traditionally in the ratio 80:20. This is the crop that has to be given the primary importance in agricultural revival.

Cotton: Though even more irrigation-dependant than wheat, it was the cash crop of the average Afghanistan farmer. The buying price used to be fixed by the government. The government set the price for cotton, and farmers allocated cropland in direct response to the government's price levels. Traditionally many farmers raised enough wheat for their own subsistence and then used the additional land for other crops such as cotton. Cotton still has a lot of potential for improvement and growth, once the water availability is assured, through the use of better newer seeds, increased fertiliser usage, both of which are linked to incentive pricing. Though this is an important crop, and its revival is very necessary, it needs to be attended to only as the third-priority crop.

Fruits and Nuts: These provided Afghanistan's traditional export crops; raisins, dried figs, almonds, and pistachios being prominent. Fresh fruits were important for sale to nearer areas, such as pre-1947 India, and later, Pakistan. The fruit production of Afghanistan was extremely important to the economy, and for years Afghanistan led the world in the export of dried fruits. Dried fruit produced in Afghanistan amounted to 60 percent of the world market in 1980, but by 1990 Afghanistan held only 16 percent of the world market. The revival of Afghanistan's orchards and the entire marketing system of fruits and dry fruits needs to be attended to as the second-priority crop sector. This is a sector in which better and more modern horticultural practices, newer varieties, and modern storage and marketing systems, including a cold chain system, can be easily incorporated. The trend towards organically-grown farm produce in the Western countries could benefit Afghanistan greatly. Quality high-value fruits, such as pomegranates, and fruit products produced by modern processing methods, could begin to transform this sector, which has much promise.

Opium Poppies, and the Eradication of Poppy Cultivation: The devastation of the Afghan countryside by war has completely altered the traditional socio-agro-economic system that existed. Other than the deliberate ruination of croplands and the destruction of the water management and irrigation regime that supported it, the war depopulated the countryside. By 1989, nine per cent of the Afghan population had been killed, 33 per cent had fled the country, and 11 per cent had become in internal refugees, mainly clustered in the urban centres. All these changes together had a two-fold effect on agriculture:

(1) It killed the possibility of labour-intensive crops, such as the plantation fruit crops, which brought in income for the larger land-holders who owned orchards, and (2) It stopped the production of cotton and of most of the country's staple, wheat. Some of the smaller farmers with a little access to water now continue to grow a little wheat, at just about a subsistence level. For the larger land-owners, who are often the tribal aristocracy, a less labour-intensive crop offered itself: the opium poppy. Some of the smaller farmers too, who could afford to spare a little irrigable land after allocating land for their basic needs of wheat, began to grow a little of this relatively hardy and easy-to-grow crop. With a profitability 250 times higher than that of other crops, poppies became the new cash crop, for richer and poorer farmers alike. By 1997 agricultural land under opium poppy cultivation had increased 1200 per cent since 1980. By 2001 Afghanistan was producing 80 per cent of the world's poppies. Only a large-scale effort to prevent poppy cultivation can free much of the presently-irrigated land for the production of other crops, for example in the best-irrigated Helmand province. International effort has been on this double-faced problem for some time, for various reasons, but only a carrot-and-stick policy which can be enforced militarily will finally allow this to happen. Since this pre-supposes a military capability to do so, it hinges on the success of the efforts to increase the Afghan government's military capacity. In the Golden Triangle area in Thailand, the Thai Government has launched a highly successful program to wean the tribal population away from opium cultivation. They were encouraged to switch from poppy to growing Mc Dermot (the most expensive variety of Almond) and Coffee. This program has been eminently successful and could form a model for Afghanistan. Alternate suggestions have been made for the Afghan government to buy up the Opium crop for sale for legitimate medical purposes. Though attractive in theory, given the conditions in Afghanistan, this could turn out to be a risky venture that could end up legitimizing the narcotics trade.

De-mining of Agricultural Land: In addition to the requirement for water, mined and otherwise damaged fields, will have to be made both safe and usable again. Repairing of terraces and other similar minor reconstruction can be undertaken the villagers once they have returned to their original homes. Removal of land-mines laid indiscriminately by various sides in the past will have to be undertaken by professionals. Some is being done by international agencies, who have engaged contractors employing ex-military men from other countries. The requirement will also need to be specifically addressed by the ANA, which will need to create the military engineer units which can continue with the task for as long as needed.

Revival of Irrigation and Overall Water Management Systems: Afghanistan is an arid or semi-arid country with insufficient and unpredictable rainfall. Consequently, irrigation has been a critical element of the Afghan economy from time immemorial, and good and effective traditional systems had been evolved over centuries. In addition to surface-water systems such as small dams, and ground-water extraction from wells, there was a well-developed gravity-fed irrigation system that utilised surface-water from snow-melt as well as precipitation, through long tunnels. This 'karez' system is very efficient, but requires constant maintenance by local labour, normally a cooperative effort by the dependant villagers, and an equitable water-distribution system, which was regulated by a Mir-e-Ab and his assistant daftary. Along with other efforts which will allow the populace to return to their villages, efforts need to be made to bring back the people with the traditional knowledge of digging and maintaining the karez. This is critical not only to re-start Afghan agriculture, but also to prevent this traditional location-specific knowledge from being lost forever. Recognizing the critical nature of water management for the well-being and growth of the country's economy, the Afghan government had promulgated a new national water management law in 1991, immediately prior to the Taliban rule. The 1991 Water Law of Afghanistan contains fifty-four articles in seven chapters and begins with a "General Provision" that seeks to ensure a sense of continuity between the new law and tradition. Along with the revival, improvement, and expansion of appropriate water technologies, traditional and modern, the new law needs to be simultaneously brought into effect.

National and International Water Law: Afghanistan is a head-water country, like Tibet, and needs to have ambitious plans to utilise the available water resources. Large countries with provinces/States that similarly are headwater States, like Colorado in the USA, have evolved legal mechanisms to resolve the water utilisation issues between upstream and lower-riparian States. In the USA, for example, the Law of Equitable Apportionment has solved this problem by applying the doctrine of prior appropriation between states that apply the law to state users. The doctrine of equitable apportionment is based on the idea that all riparian States must perpetually share the use of a watercourse. This allows a slower-developing State to put its waters to use at any time it chooses and places a very high burden on downstream States who object to the new diversion. However, internal laws such as this do not apply to sovereign nations, and Iran, the Central Asian countries, and Pakistan, to which Afghanistan's rivers flow, are likely to raise objections to Afghanistan's plans. Internationally, restricted sovereignty or equitable utilization is the applicable norm for internationally-shared waters. Afghanistan today is a creature of its European and United States donors, donor agencies, and the UN, and will therefore also have to be subject to world environmental laws on water use. Afghanistan's needs for expanded water come at a time when international water law is evolving from its historical function of storage and diversion promotion. The international legal regimc is slowly evolving toward a more ecologically balanced regime which gives more weight to the conservation of the integrity of aquatic ecosystems and the maintenance of flow regimes that more closely approximate a river's pre-human intervention hydrograph. Foreign funding will force Afghanistan to use water more efficiently and to engage in watershed management and integrated basin planning.

Helmand Valley Project: An ambitious project for integrated basin planning had been planned and begun in the 1950s, for specifically the same purposes as mentioned above. It was modelled on the USA's Tennessee Valley project, which set up the well-known Tennessee Valley Authority (TVA). The Helmand Valley Project (HVP), was a project involving foreign funding, from the USA, and a foreign overall contractor, also from the USA. The project soaked up all the money, but failed to achieve its objectives, leaving the Afghan educated classes disillusioned with the USA. The problem in part was that it was over-ambitious. It was so big that it absorbed practically all of the educated people of Afghanistan, which had a negative impact on the administration and development of the rest of Afghan society. This is being brought out to highlight the fact that the problems of Afghan economic growth are not new, they are well-understood, and attempts have been made before to surmount them. That they have not succeeded is due to other weaknesses and shortcomings in Afghanistan's political existence and its administrative system, as well as corruption in both high and low places. The attempts made before need to be known and understood, so that the implementation errors are not repeated.

Revival of the Livestock Economy: In 1976 livestock products accounted for seven per cent of Afghanistan's GDP and 15 per cent of its exports, which included both the famed Karakul sheepskins and live sheep to Iran. Sheep herding and goat herding were the largest forms of livestock production in Afghanistan. Herding was undertaken largely by the nomadic peoples of the country. The Afghan nomads were thought to own 80 percent of the twenty million sheep and 3.3 million goats. This provided them the financial stability that form of life requires. For the settled farmers too, small numbers of livestock raised as a small side-line represented disposable cash income. In any case, in the agricultural areas, some cattle are required for drought purposes for normal farming operations, tractors being feasible only in a more modern economy. The livestock sector in Afghanistan has suffered a serious set-back through the war decades, and needs to be revitalised for socio-economic reasons.

RESUMPTION OF LOCAL AND INTERNATIONAL TRADE

Though this is a vast subject by itself, it will be only briefly touched upon here. Trade is always contingent upon peaceful conditions, except for the clandestine and generally illegal businesses that thrive in war-time anywhere. The first requirement, therefore, is internal political stability with no violent upheavals. Obviously, this situation will only come about when a successful political formula for governance has been arrived at, and uncertainty ends, and when there is a peaceful law-and-order situation in the towns and cities and along the highways. It is assumed that it is possible to have the second without the first, as long as the ANA and police are strong enough, and simultaneously also have the support of foreign troops, even if only for urban peace-keeping purposes.

It is possible, therefore, for enough trade to resume to help the local economy and, though slowly, for organised international trade in local produce to begin. What is needed is to create enough confidence in the trading community to return and resume their old businesses, and to rebuild markets, such as the mandis that used to function. These measures do not require elaboration here.

The related issue is to restore the old faith-based '*hundi*' system which was common to India and Afghanistan in pre-partition days, and which continues to some extent within India even today. Creating a favourable micro-credit scheme at the national level, through a local banking system that gives traders some financial leeway, will help kick-start local markets. International trading will require banking to be integrated into the world-wide banking system, with the availability of Bank Guarantees (BG) and Letters of Credit (LCs) to enable exports from Afghanistan to pick up again. The old traditional trading credit '*hundi*' system of India extended as far as the Persian Gulf till fairly recent times, and to Afghanistan pre-partition. It may not be possible to impose international '*hundi*' linkages by government diktat, but traders are very practical people, and the system could well revive on its own, once trade linkages resume.

The entire economy of Afghanistan also needs a local banking sytem that can integrate with the larger national one, to reduce the tyranny of money-lenders. To make this popular, it needs to be made to incorporate 'Islamic banking' practices, i.e. become 'Sharia-compliant'[1]. This is particularly necessary in traditional rural and small-town Afghanistan, in order to prevent the fundamentalists (the mullahs and the Taliban) from taking the moral high ground against modern banking. Social banking, therefore, within reason, is a national need for the country. In addition, a system such as Bangladesh's famous '*Grameen*' Bank, should also be initiated. International financial institutions need to be sensitised to these practical requirements, so that a corpus be can arranged for the national bank.

Finally, no Afghanistan government can survive if it cannot raise taxes from its populace. There is no doubt that this requires a 'social contract', as explained by Hobbes, Rosseau, and Locke. In Afghanistan, however, this will be impossible to expect in the present context. It has been described as 'a Country without a State', and to modern European eyes that is what it seems. Afghanistan is still in a medieval mindset in this respect, and the only way to realise taxes is the medieval way. As had been noted by Babur in the context of Afghanistan, when he personally ruled there from AD 1504-1525, tax can be 'either of the sword or of the pen', i.e., collected by force, or on the basis of a written assessment that is agreed to by the locals being taxed. This principle was well-known in India till the British Empire had captured all of India and proved too strong for Indians to resist. The Marathas, two centuries later, who were the predominant power in India till the British, collected taxes of a quarter of the produce, or *'chauth'*, on exactly the same principle described by Babur. Either the '*zamindar*' paid the annual tax as assessed by the Maratha tax-collecting official, or had to later face a Maratha army who would collect it with arrears. It is not surprising that the British named their land-records department in India the 'Revenue' department, as it is still known today. Even today, the local '*Kanungo*' and the '*Patwari*' visit villages twice a year in India, for the '*girdawri*', once after the *Kharif* crop, and once after the Rabi crop, to assess the taxation. Afghanistan today is not at a stage where land-produce tax can be collected from individuals through their village headmen 'by the pen'. It will need to be collected by the Provincial Governors from the villages, but the Afghanistan government will have to take it, or have to create the military capability to take it, 'by the threat of use of force'. It should clearly be borne in mind however that the ANA is presently very far from such a capability and presently has its hands full fighting the Taliban insurgency. It would be well beyond its existing capability to effect a major shift in the tax recovery base or capacity. Modern banking systems linked to international financial institutions can help, but without collection of taxes from the provinces, the central government itself cannot stabilise.

MINERALS

Copper: Afghanistan is fairly rich in minerals. These could provide a significant route for the recovery of the Afghan economy and merit serious attention. Afghanistan has significant deposits of Copper. The Chinese are already developing the 28 square km Aynak Copper field in the Logar province. This is stated to have up to 88 billion $ worth of ore and is likely to yield a royalty of 400 million $ a year. The Chinese are building a power plant and will construct a railroad to carry off the ore to China. It is noteworthy that the Chinese demand for Copper had risen by 35% in 2007 alone.

Other Minerals: Afghanistan has large Iron ore deposits in Herat and Panjshir. Chinese demand for Iron had risen by 15% in2007and they would be keen to exploit this resource. India could assist in the development of the Heart Iron ore deposits due to their proximity to Iran. Besides, there are Gold deposits in the Northern Provinces of Badakshan, Takhar and Ghazni. Since India is a major exporter of Gold ornaments it could explore possibilities in this sector. Besides, Afghanistan has appreciable deposits of Coal, Chromite, Talc, Sulphur, Lead, Zinc as well as precious and semi-precious stones. It is noteworthy that most of these mineral deposits are in the relatively more peaceful Northern provinces that are feeling let down by India in the post-Taliban scenario. India now needs to redress this perception by undertaking extensive development in the Northern Provinces where execution of projects will be far easier.

Natural Gas and Oil: Afghanistan has some 49.55 million Cubic meters of gas deposits. Prior to the Soviet invasion, Natural Gas export revenues were of the order of 300 million $ per year. These were exported primarily to Russia. Due to the fighting these gas fields were capped. These need to be revived and pipeline infrastructures created for their export. In fact Natural Gas exports could provide a very viable pathway for the economic revival of the Afghan state and also generate employment. Recent American geological surveys have revised Natural Gas reserve estimates for Afghanistan by three times. Similarly, oil reserves estimates for Afghanistan have been revised upwards by a factor of 15 (to 1596 million barrels). It is noteworthy that currently

Afghanistan imports its entire needs of oil. Exploitation of Afghanistan's mineral resource could go a very long way towards reviving the Afghan economy in a sustainable manner so that over time, it can sustain itself without a heavy dependence on continued foreign aid. What is cause for optimism is the fact that the bulk of these mineral deposits are in the Northern provinces that have not been affected so much by the Taliban insurgency. India- Afghanistan trade was worth 216 million US$ in 2006-07. This is expected to rise to over a billion US$ in the next five years. Indian firms must be encouraged and facilitated to invest in Afghanistan. To start with, they could focus on projects in the more stable and peaceful Northern Provinces, and thereafter extend their areas of operations to the East and South.

MILITARY CONSOLIDATION

Just as there can be no state without state power, there can be no state power without state-owned and controlled armed forces. In Afghanistan, unfortunately, state power has not always been available in sufficient amount. This is primarily because Afghanistan, as presently geographically constituted, is a country which inherited the boundaries of a former kingdom. The kingdom of Amir Abdur Rehman established what are almost the boundaries of modern Afghanistan, except for the loss of its Eastern Pathan-inhabited mountains, first to British India and then to Pakistan. It was because of the strength of arms that he managed to establish his rule over the non-Pathan areas north of the Hindu Kush Mountains, and right up to the Amu Darya (River). Had the Emir of Bukhara possessed the necessary military strength at the time to effectively contest his bringing under the Uzbek, Turkmen, and Tajik-inhabited areas south of the river, Abdur Rehman's kingdom may have been smaller. The '*Loya Jirga*' which made Abdur Rehman king might not have received such assent from the non-Pathan leaders had they not been mindful of his army. Thus it can be seen that a 'social contract' for a monarchy was established under the shadow of a threat of armed might.

The kingdom's boundaries were allowed to continue due to their convenience for the Russian Empire in the north and the British Indian Empire in the east.[2] Owing to the mix of ethnicities within these boundaries, Afghanistan is not a 'nation-state'[3] in any sense of the word. It thus has an underlying problem of legitimacy even for its own inhabitants. This lies at the root of the many political problems it continuously faces. The State, therefore, has to maintain its 'legal' position by the implied threat of armed action, if it is to govern effectively.

Parliamentary Democratic Afghanistan Government: If Afghanistan is to be a democratic form of government, then armed action against its citizens is going to be an unlikely or even impossible tasking for the ANA. If political dissent means either armed rebellion or non-compliance, then theoretically the ANA might have to fight the rebels either conventionally or as COIN operations. Neither will be possible under a democracy. COIN operations require a very large army to pacify large spaces, by occupying them with a COIN-grid. An army of the required size would be unaffordable for the economy of Afghanistan at the best of times. Nor would it be operationally possible for any 'national' army composed of citizens voluntarily recruited in an army with proportional representation for each of its ethnic groups. Even otherwise, the cost of a large and powerful army can only be borne by a State that collects enough money to afford the requisite size of army, and for a democracy this will be a Catch-22 situation. No taxes, no strong central government; no government, no army; no army, no taxes.

Presidential Semi-Democratic Government: Under a presidential form of government, there is greater likelihood of a strong enough ANA whose presence will allow the government to govern. It tasking will have to be both punitive and enforcement of the taxation regime. Unlike an army expected to carry out a COIN task, such an army can be organised to be much smaller in numbers, but much more lethal in hitting power against recalcitrant communities. It would also need some conventional warfare capability, given that Pakistan can easily supply tanks and other armoured vehicles to its rebel surrogates. Therefore, such an ANA will need to be reasonably modern in terms of armament and other equipment, have sufficient anti-tank capability as well as modern manouevre-warfare elements, such as a small bit modern aroured corps with both tanks and mechanised nfantry combat vehicles (MICVs). An air arm will also be necessary, for close air support (CAS) tasks, with aircraft such as the US A-10 Warthog being the aircraft of choice. Helicopter support is needed for a certain amount of infantry or Special Forces heli-lift capability, and some Air Observation Post aircraft, both helicopter and fixed-wing for the direction of artillery fire.

Punitive actions will be difficult to carry out with a 'national'-type army. It is recommended that the combat arms be created on a 'single-class' or 'fixed-class' basis, so as to prevent the social and organizational problems of troops having to attack their own villages or immediate home region. The British in India evolved the Indian Army to control India, on the 'class' system, after a hundred years of trial and error from 1757 to 1857, with further refinements in 1903 and 1922. On the other hand, the 'national army'-type of class composition would be ideal for the engineer units which are primarily going to be used for de-mining of croplands and other re-construction tasks. It would also be ideal for the medical corps and other services.

Finally, it needs to be borne in mind that Afghanistan's size, ethno-political complexities, and the anticipated size of its economy cannot support the size of ANA that is needed. Neither can the planned 134,000-strong ANA and the foreign forces likley to be deployed in 2009 together make any impact if they are to fight anti-national elements as COIN operations. A re-think on the tasking and operational philosophy, and the appropriate size of the ANA is required, if the military consolidation of Afghanistan is desired.

Right-Sizing the ANA: It needs to be borne in mind that prior to the Soviet invasion, the Afghan Army had a strength of 350,000 with 12 infantry divisions, three tank and three commando brigades. This was depleted to just 30,000 due to large scale desertions. The Soviets invested heavily in recreating the Afghan Army and the Secret Service (the Khad). By 1987 they had raised it to an impressive figure of 550,000. This refurbished Army had five corps and was very well equipped to Soviet standards. What is significant is the fact that it performed very well in combat. In fact this Afghan Army held out with ease against the Mujahideen for over three years. It beat back repeated attacks on Jalalabad and effectively defended Kabul and other key Afghan cities. It unraveled not as a result of the military pressure of the Mujahideen but because the Soviets pulled out the economic plug and stopped paying this Army or the Jowzjani Militia of Abdul Rashid Dostam. A viable Afghan Army therefore will have to be far bigger than the 134,000 strong, straight legged Infantry force that the Americans have envisaged for Afghanistan. To win the war against the Taliban the optimal size of the ANA would have to be in the region of 500,000 strong. Once the military situation is stabilized, the pre Soviet- era Army of 350,000 may suffice. The weak ANA, as presently structured, amounts merely to tokenism. It could at best hold on for a year or two, post the US withdrawal. To ensure the stabilisation of a viable nation state in Afghanistan, the international community will perforce have to make a heavy investment in raising and initially sustaining sufficiently capable armed forces that can quell the Taliban insurgency and guarantee the sovereignty of this recreated state. The Rentier state argument cannot be stretched beyond a point. The fact is that between 1919 and the Soviet invasion in 1979, a largely self-sustaining state had functioned in Afghanistan for almost seven decades. This buffer state was comprehensively destroyed by the conflict between the two superpowers in which Pakistan played a key role in facilitating the destruction of the oldest nation state in recent Asian history. It would be in the interests of global peace and security to ensure that no ungoverned space exists in the Asian heartland. That will be extremely destabilizing for Central and South Asia in particular and the world in general. 9/11 bears testimony to how dangerous myopic and short-sighted strategies of historic revenge can prove to be. In rooting for the Taliban, Pakistan, in fact, is trying to prevent the consolidation of this rival state and reduce it to the status of a perennially ungoverned space.

Notes:

- Globally accepted regulatory agencies that can assist and check compliance are the Islamic Financial Services Board and the Accounting and Auditing Organisation for Islamic Financial Instiutions. The basic principles of finance under Sharia Law are: Prohibits any transaction that involves paying interest.

- Bans investment in certain sectors such as gambling and prostitution.
- Thc investor and the recipient must shatre any risk.
- Transactions have to be underpinned by tangible assets.
- The eastern boundary was pushed closer to Kabul by the Durand Line agreement of 1893, supposedly for a period of 100 years.
- It is worth noting that Pakistan was created on the basis of a 'two-nation' theory postulating that the Hindus and Muslims of India constituted two separate 'nations'.

REFERENCES

1. Ahmed, Ali, "Afghanistan: A Strategic Assessment," *War College Journal,* Vol 37, No 02, Autumn 2008, pp. 56-61.
2. Anderson, John Ward, "8 Afghan Truisms," Capitol News Company, LLC, February 22, 2009.
3. Anderson, I.M., "Rehabilitation of Informal Irrigation in Afghanistan," FAO, 1993.
4. Anderson, I.M., "Irrigation systems, Water Management, Livestock and the Opium Economy," (Kabul, Afghanistan Research & Evaluation Unit), 2006.
5. Babur, Zahir-uddin Muhammad, "Babur Nama" (The Journal of Emperor Babur) (AD 1483-1530), translated from the Chagtai Turki by Anette Susannah Beveridge, New Delhi, Penguin Books India, 2006.
6. Bakshi, G.D., "Afghanistan: The Next Faultline War," New Delhi, Lancers Publishers, 19?? .
7. Basu Roy, Arpita, "Afghanistan: Towards a Viable State," Gurgaon, Hope India Publications, 2002.
8. Bonsle, Rahul K., "The Impact of Geo-Politics of Southwest Asia on Afghanistan: A MediumTermPerspective," Centre for Land Warfare Studies, 2008.
9. Caroe, Olaf. 2000 (reprint of 1958 edition). *The Pathans: 500 B.C.-A.D. 1957.* London: Kegan Paul International.
10. Celerier, Pierre, "Drought Threatens Afghan Irrigation," in *The Dawn Internet Edition,* Jul 20, 2002.
11. Chan, Samuel. 2007. "Sentinels of Afghan Democracy: The Afghan National Army," S.
12. Rajaratnam School of International Studies Working Paper No. 128. Online: http://www.rsis.edu.sg/publications/WorkingPapers/WP128.pdf
13. Chandra, Vishal, "Politics in Post-Taliban Afghanistan: An Assessment," *Strategic Analysis,* Vol. 29, No. 2, Apr-Jun 2005, pp. 222-249.
14. Chandra, Vishal, "Talking to the Taliban," *Strategic Analysis,* Vol. 32 , No. 5, September 2008, pp. 729-737.

15. Chandra, Vishal, "Making of the New Afghan Army: Challenges and Prospects," *Strategic Analysis,* Vol 33, No 1, January 2009, pp. 55-70.

16. Chandra, Vishal, "The National front in Afghan Politics: An Exploratory Study," *Strategic Analysis,* Vol. 33, No. 4, July 2009, pp. 528-540.

17. Cordesman, Anthony H. 2007, "Armed Nation Building: The Real Challenge in Afghanistan," CSIS. http://www.csis.org/media/csis/pubs/071107_afghanchall.pdf Fick, Nathaniel C., John A. Nagl. 2009. "Counterinsurgency Field Manual: Afghanistan Edition," Foreign Policy, Jan./Feb. Online: http://www.foreignpolicy.com/story/cms.php?story_id=4587

18. Gauster, Markus. 2008. "Provincial Reconstruction Teams in Afghanistan," Marshall European Center for Security Studies. Occasional Paper #16 (January 2008). Online: http://www.marshallcenter.org/site-graphic/lang-en/page-pubs-index-1/static/xdocs/research/static/occpapers/occ-paper_16-en.pdf.

19. Giustozzi, Antonio. 2002. "Afghanistan: The Problems of Creating a New Afghan army and the critical dangers of failure!" *International Industrial Information* (April 2002). http://www.newnations.com/specialreports/pdf/af.01.04.03.pdf

20. Giustozzi, Antonio. 2007. "Auxiliary Force or National Army? Afghanistan's 'ANA' and the Counter-Insurgency Effort, 20022006," *Small Wars and Insurgencies,* Vol. 18, No. 1 4567, March 2007.

21. Giustozzi, Antonio. 2003. "Military Reform in Afghanistan," pp. 23-32 in Brief 28. Confronting Afghani'tan's Security Dilemma: Reforming the Security Sector, Mark Sedra (ed.). Bonn International Center for Conversion, September 2003. Online: http://www.bicc.de/publications/briefs/brief28/brief28.pdf

22. Goswami, Namrata, "The Obama Administration's Afghanistan-Pakistan Policy in Need of an Urgent Rethink," *Strategic Analysis,* Vol. 33, No. 4, July 2009, pp. 465-469.

23. Grace, Jo and Adam Pain. 2004. "Rethinking Rural Livelihoods in Afghanistan," AREU.http://www.areu.org.af/index.php?option=com_docman&Itemid=&task=doc_download&gid=319

24. Groh, Ty L. 2006. "Ungoverned Spaces: the Challenges of Governing Tribal Societies," Naval Postgraduate School Thesis. Monterey, California (June 2006). http://handle.dtic.mil/100.2/ADA451373

25. Gujja, Biksham, "Healing Afghanistan," *Down to Earth,* Vol. 11, Issue 20020930

26. Herold, Marc W., "Afghan Tragedy," *Frontline,* July 3, 2009, pp. 4-14.

27. Hope, Ian. 2008. "Unity of Command in Afghanistan: A Forsaken Principle of War," US Army War College. Online: http://handle.dtic.mil/100.2/ADA482251.

28. Huber, Jeff, "Our Mc Man in Bananastan," *Pen and Sword: Jeff Huber,* June 04, 2009, on the Internet at http://zenhuber.blogspot.com/ accessed on June 21, 2009.

29. International Legal Foundation. 2004. "The Customary Laws of Afghanistan," The International Legal Foundation, September 2004. Available at: http://www.usip.org/ruleoflaw/projects/ilf_customary_law_afghanistan.pdf

30. Jalalzai, Musa Khan, "Afghan National Army: State Security, Nuclear Neighbours and Internal Security Threats," Lahore, Al-Abbas International, 2004/2005.

31. Johnson, Thomas H. 2007. "On the Edge of the Big Muddy: The Taliban Resurgence in Afghanistan," *China and Eurasia Forum Quarterly*, Vol. 5, No. 2 (2007). Online:
http://www.silkroadstudies.org/new/docs/CEF/Quarterly/May_2007/Johnson.pdf
32. Joshi, A., "Afghanistan: History, Taliban, Operation Enduring Freedom and New Challeges," U.S.I. *Journal*, Vol. CXXXII, No. 549, July-September 2002, pp. 314-328.
33. Loo, Jonathan, "The Performance of Community Water Management Systems," (Kabul, Afghanistan Research & Evaluation Unit), 2007.
34. Lyon, Peter David Sterling, 2007, "A solution for ethnic conflict: democratic governance in Afghanistan, a case study," Thesis (M.A.)—University of Manitoba. Online:
http://www.collectionscanada.ca/obj/s4/f2/dsk3/MWU/TC-MWU-298.pdf
35. Mahmood, Tariq, 2005, "The Durand Line: South Asia's new trouble spot," Thesis (M.A. in National Security Affairs)—Naval Postgraduate School (U.S.). Online:
http://www.ccc.nps.navy.mil/research/theses/Mahmood05.pdf
36. McMurray, James C., and A. Dan Tarlock, "The Law of Later-Developing Riparian States: The Case of Afghanistan," Colloquium Articles, *N.Y.U. Environmental Law Journal*, Vol. 12, 2005, pp. 711-763.
37. Millen, Raymond. 2005. "Afghanistan: reconstituting a collapsed state," *Strategic Studies*Institute. Available online at:
http://www.carlisle.army.mil/ssi/pdffiles/PUB600.pdf
38. Miller, Laura and Robert Perito. 2004. "Establishing the Rule of Law in Afghanistan," United States Institute of Peace Special Report #117. March 2004. Available at:
http://www.hdcentre.org/datastore/USIP%20Afghanistan%20ROL%20 Report.pdf
39. Mukherjee, Ranjana, et al. 2007. "Afghanistan, Building an Effective State: Priorities for Public Administration Reform," World Bank Report. Online:
http://www.reliefweb.int/rw/rwb.nsf/db900sid/LSGZ -7FGHWZ/$File/full_report.pdf
40. Noelle-Karimi, Christine and Conrad Schetter and Reinhard Schlagintweit (editors) 2002, "Afghanistan—A Country without a State?," Frankfurt am Main, Germany: IKO- Verlag fur Interkulturelle Kommunikation.
41. Pain, Adam and Sue Lautze. 2002. "Addressing Livelihoods in Afghanistan," AREU.
http://www.areu.org.af/index.php?option=com_docman&Itemid=&task=doc_download&gid=264
42. Parris, Matthew, "In the fog, remember: victory is impossible in Afghansitan," London, The Times Online, July 4, 2009, on the Internet at
http://www.timesonline.co.uk/tol/comment/columnists/matthew_parris/ article6632876.ece, accessed on July 21, 2009

43. Paterson, Anna. 2006. "Putting the Cart Before the Horse? Privatisation and Economic Reform in Afghanistan," AREU. Online: http://www.areu.org.af/index.php?option=com_docman&Itemid=&task =doc_download&gid=458
44. Pomper, US Army Major Stephen D. 2005. "Don't Follow the Bear: The Soviet Attempt to Build Afghanistan's Military," *Military Review,* (Sept.-Oct. 2005). http://usacac.army.mil/CAC/milreview/English/SepOct05/SEPOCT05/ pomper.pdf
45. Qureshi, Asad Sarwar, "Water Resources Management in Afghanistan: The Issues and Options," IWMI, Working Paper 49 http://www.cawater-info.net/afgaistan/afg_8e.htm
46. "Rebuilding Karez" in Catchwater, The CSE Campaign for People's Water Management, Vol 4, No 5, Oct-Nov 200
47. Rhyne, Richard G. Jr. 2004, "Special Forces command and control in Afghanistan," Thesis (MMAS)U.S. Army Command and General Staff College (CGSC). Online: http://cgsc.cdmhost.com/u?/p4013coll2,249.
48. Rogers, Bruce, Jim Hope and Robert Kemp. 2008. "PRTs in Afghanistan: A report from the inside," *Foreign Service Journal,* Vol. 85, No. 7. Online: http://www.afsa.org/fsj/julaug08/prts.pdf
49. Rout, Bob, "How the Water Flows: A Typology of Irrigation Systems in Afghanistan," (Kabul, Afghanistan Research & Evaluation Unit), 2008.
50. Rubin, Barnett R., "The Fragmentation of Afghanistan: State Formation and Collapse in the International System," New Haven and London, 1995.
51. Rubin, Barnett R. 2009, "The Transformation of the Afghan State," in The Future of Afghanistan, edited by J. Alexander Thier. United States Institute of Peace. Online: http://www.usip.org/peaceops/afghanistan/foa.pdf
52. Samay Ram, "The New Afghanistan: Pawn of America," New Delhi, Manas Publications, 2004.
53. Sawhney, R.K., "In Search of a New Strategy in Afghanistan," *CLAWS Issue Brief,* No 8, April 2009.
54. Schetter, Conrad. 2002. "Challenging the warlord culture: security sector reform in post- Taliban Afghanistan," BICC Paper #25. Available online at: http://www.bicc.de/publications/papers/paper25/paper25.pdf
55. Schetter, Conrad, Rainer Glassner and Masood Karokhail. 2007. "Beyond Warlordism: The local Security Architecture in Afghanistan," *Internationale Politik und Gesellschaft* 2:136-153: http://www.fes.de/IPG/inhalt_d/pdf/10_Schetter_US.pdf
56. Scott, Trent and John Agoglia. 2008. "Getting the Basics Right: A Discussion on Tactical Actions for Strategic Impact in Afghanistan, Small Wars Journal. http://smallwarsjournal.com/mag/docs-temp/134-scott-agoglia.pdf
57. Sellers, Cameron S. 2007. "Provincial Reconstruction Teams: Improving Effectiveness," Naval Postgraduate School Master's Thesis. Online: http://handle.dtic.mil/100.2/ADA474498

58. Shahrani, M. Nazif. 2001. "Resisting the Taliban and Talibanism in Afghanistan: Legacies of a Century of Internal Colonialism and Cold War Politics in a Buffer State," *Perceptions: Journal of International Affairs,* 5(4). Available online at: www.sam.gov.tr/perceptions/Volume5/Dec2000-Feb2001/VolumeVN4RESISTINGTHETALIBANANDTALIBANISMINAFGHANISTAN.pdf
59. Spain, James, W., "The Way of the Pathans," Karachi, Oxford University Press, 1962, 2nd Ed. 1972.
60. Manner, Stephen. 2002. "Afghanistan: A Military History from Alexander the Great to the Fall of the Taliban," Cambridge, MA: Da Capo Press.
61. Temperate Fruit and Nut Production (HORT 319), FAO, 2001.
62. Uma Shankar, "State Building in Afghanistan: Linkages with International Politics," Delhi, Academic Excellence, 2008.
63. Yousaf, Mohammed, and Mark Adkin, "The Bear Trap: Afghanistan's Untold Story," Lahore, Jang Publishers, 1992.
64. Zakhilwal, Omar, The Helmand Valley Project, Institute for Afghan Studies, on the Internet at http://www.institute-for-afghan-studies.org/Foreign%20Affairs/us-afghan/helmand_0.htm, accessed on June 03, 2009.

8

India's Options and Strategies

THE STRATEGIC SCENARIO: END STATES AND OUTCOMES

India's options and response strategies would emanate from an understanding/estimation of which way the Strategic Scenario could unfold in this region. This has been attempted in an empirical fashion in this study by outlining alternative Military, Political and Economic futures for Afghanistan. Before outlining India's options and strategies it would be essential to first summarize the emerging Strategic Scenario in this region.

The Short Term Scenario: Given the fluidity of the situation, it would be essential first to focus on the short term/near term scenario that could emerge from a success or otherwise of the American surge in Afghanistan. Three end states were visualized for this surge over the time horizon of the next three to four years:

- *Stay the Course:* An optimistic scenario where the US surge succeeds (without incurring heavy casualties). This encourages the US and NATO countries to stay the course (with existing force levels) for armed nation state building process that could last from one to two decades.
- *Thin Out Scenario:* US surge is partially successful but entails heavy casualties that increase political costs. Accordingly in 2011 President Obama declares victory and begins to thin out ground troops presence. However Air power and Special Forces are retained in an 'over watch' role.
- *Precipitate Withdrawal Scenario:* This would largely be an outgrowth of scenario two. It would be premised upon a relative failure of the surge in Afghanistan and a recrusedence of Pakistani Taliban in the NWFP and FATA regions of Pakistan. If heavy casualties are

sustained by US/NATO forces in Afghanistan, political pressure to wind down the operations in Afghanistan could mount . Overtime it could degenerate into a Precipitate Withdrawal Scenario (especially, if other crises situation emerge in North East/ South East Asia that demand US attention and resources). This could occur in a time horizon of five to six years. The underlying scenario logic is premised on the palpable weakness of the ANA that will not be able to sustain operations in a stand alone mode post a US withdrawal, beyond one to two years at best.

THE LONG TERM STRATEGIC SCENARIO

The outcome of the short term scenarios would influence the way the long term strategic scenario in this region unfolds over the next 10-15 years time horizon. The possible end states/outcomes in the longer term horizon could be as under:

- *Stabilisation of Nation State in Afghanistan:* The long term success of armed nation state building could lead to the stabilisation of a relatively modernist and inclusive state in Afghanistan.
- *Ethnic Fragmentation:* The Taliban had practiced politics of ethnic exclusion and carried out ethnic cleansing of the Uzbeks and Hazaras in the campaign for subjugating the whole of Afghanistan (1995-96). This has sharply polarized the issue of ethnic identities in Afghanistan. The current Karzai administration is making a concerted attempt to downplay ethnic identities and revise a pan-Afghan nationalism by establishing a highly centralised state under a Presidential system. The present state institutions are fragile and overly dependent upon one or two charismatic individuals with a pan Afghan acceptance. Pakistan's ISI has consciously tried to subsume Afghan nationalism by prompting a Salafi-Sunni ideology. It has been trying to gain depth in Afghanistan by promoting the Taliban and using it for acquiring the Pashtun areas of Afghanistan. A Taliban ascendance could certainly lead to a fragmentation of Afghanistan along ethnic faultlines. The possible outcomes of these contra-trends could be as under:

- Ethnic Fragmentation Afghan State fractures along the Pashtun-Farsiwan fault line due to Taliban domination.
- Taliban's Pashtun Consolidation Pakistan assumes de-facto control of the Pashtun areas of Afghanistan via the instrumentality of the Taliban. Pakistan thus expands territorially and gains its long cherished strategic depth in Afghanistan at the cost of splintering that nation state.

"Pashtun Khwa": Given the intensity of Pashtun sentiments aroused by Pakistan's participation in the GWOT (and the increasing irrelevance of the Durand Line) the reverse could happen and a new Pashtun entity that straddles the Durand Line could emerge as a state (Pashtun Khwa). This would emerge at the cost of the fragmentation of Pakistan along the Indus faultline. The capital of such a Pashtun entity may well be Peshawar and not Kabul (that lies far to the North in non-Pashtun territory). Alternatively a Pashtun Khwa could emerge even as a nation state stabilizes in Afghanistan and the Pashtun tribes in the NWFP and FATA seek merger with Afghanistan.

The Question of Baluchistan: The Baloch people (like the Kurds) are spread over the territories of three states (Iran, Pakistan and Afghanistan). The Baloch Insurgency in Pakistan is very old and had flared up in a major way in 1974. It is once again on the rise. The Jundollah, a Baloch insurgent organisation, is active in Iran's Eastern province of Sistan (reportedly with CIA support). The strategic significance of Balochistan, stems from its mineral resources (especially Natural Gas) and the important ports of Gwadar and Chahbahar in Baloch ethnic areas. China has plans to develop the Gwadar Port as a major Naval Base and transportation hub that helps it to bypass the bottle neck or the choke point of the Malacca Straits. The Americans obviously would not like to let the Chinese acquire a Naval base on the Makran Coast and dominate the vital Persian Gulf sea lanes. The CIA is supporting the Jundollah to destabilize Iranian Balochistan (Sistan). Because of the significant clash of interests of major powers like USA and China in Balochistan, this region could witness significant turbulence. If the Pakistani state fractures along the Pashtun faultline of the Indus, Balochistan could well be the next ethnic entity to break away from Pakistan.

Therefore in the long term the key questions are:

- Would the Afghan nation state stabilize in its existing form or would it fall to the Taliban?
- Would that lead to its breakup along ethnic faultlines (with/without a complete take over by the Taliban)?
- In such a scenario which way will the Pashtun entity go? Will Pakistan take control of the Pashtun population on both sides of the Durand Line through the instrumentality of the Taliban?
- Conversely could Pashtun angst against Pakistan for its support to the GWOT, lead to the secession of the Pashtun parts of Pakistan to form a new Trans- Durand line Pashtun entity (PashtunKhwa)? In a situation of ethnic conflict, this entity could well relocate its capital to Peshawar rather than Kabul.

In devising responses and strategies, India would have to carefully analyse the impact of each of these scenarios on its security.

- The best case scenario from the Indian point of view would be if the present state of Afghanistan survives and stabilizes in an even more ethnically inclusive form that is durable/stable overtime.
- The worst case scenario would be a Taliban consolidation over the whole/Pashtun part of Afghanistan.

India's Aim: India's aim simply should be to ensure that Afghanistan is not controlled or dominated by any power hostile to India. Towards that end India should work towards the following:

- Help to stabilize an independent and relatively modernist nation state in Afghanistan.
- Try to prevent the takeover of this country by the fundamentalist Taliban.
- Assist the Afghan state by capacity building of its armed forces and state institutions and a revival of its Agricultural economy and educational sectors.

DIPLOMATIC STRATEGIES

- India needs to be far more proactive in engaging Iran, Russia and the Central Asian States. In the event of any US/NATO withdrawal it should press for a regional initiative to support the existing state in Afghanistan.

- It should encourage the US/ ISAF to stay engaged for the long haul to ensure the stabilisation of the state in Afghanistan. It should press for greater role for Regional States .
- It should encourage NATO/EU countries that have better relations with Iran to use the Bandar Abbas and Chahbahar routes for logistical support of their forces in Afghanistan. This will provide an alternative supply route via Iran and thereby reduce Pakistan's leverage
- India must insist that the US should give this country a far larger diplomatic profile in forging a regional consensus on Afghanistan The outcome in Afghanistan has serious security implications for the region. So far the American Af-Pak package has focused primarily on the carrots and not the disincentives that could discourage the Military-ISI complex in Pakistan from using non-state actors to destabilize its neighbours and pursue the GWOT with greater vigour and sincerity.
- *Inclusive Strategy:* Need to engage the US on the issue of Afghanistan. If it feels its NATO allies are not doing enough it could involve regional actors like Iran and Central Asia and even moderate Muslim states like Egypt and Jordon. India has as much, if not a greater stake in Afghanistan than France or Germany.
- *Free Trade and Transit:* Afghanistan is now a member of the SAARC and SAFTA. Pakistan must be pressurised to give transit for Indian aid and trade for Afghanistan. The Law of the Sea permits landlocked states the right of access to the Sea. Pakistan has been leveraging this issue of access to the sea to force Afghanistan into a dependency situation. Hence its opposition to India developing communication infrastructure to link the Afghan road network with Iran's.
- Pakistan's strategy has been to subsume Afghan nationalism with the ideology of Jihad premised upon Salafi/Wahabi extremism. It is seeking to control the Pashtun areas of Afghanistan through the instrumentality of the Taliban. In a multi-ethnic society, the Taliban

has tried in the past to enforce mono-ethnic domination and even carried out ethnic cleansing of the Uzbeks and Hazaras during its first campaign for the consolidation of Afghanistan. A Taliban resurgence in Afghanistan therefore could again lead to politics of ethnic exclusion that could result in a fragmentation of the country. It would be in India's interests to prevent a Taliban reconsolidation in that state.

- Pakistan's strategy is a zero- sum game that seeks to destabilize all its neighbours to gain competitive advantage and expand territorial depth/control water resources. Its constant attempts to alter the status quo by employing non-state actors for asymmetric warfare against virtually all its neighbours, has destabilized the whole region. The blow back effect on its own polity is now clearly visible. Disincentives must be created to induce Pakistan to change this disastrous course.
- *Durand Line/LC Linkage:* Ever since the First Indo-Pak war of 1947-48, Pakistan has constantly questioned J&Ks accession to India and refused to respect the LC. It has for the past two decades been infiltrating terrorists across the LC to destabilize the state. India could retaliate by supporting the Pashtun demand for a reopening of the issue of the Durand Line. De-facto this line no longer is a functional /effective boundary.
- *Political Evolution of the Afghan State:* The Constitutional Loya Jirga (CLJ) was almost deadlocked in 2004 over the basic issue of whether Afghanistan should have a Centralised Presidential form of Government or a Federal Parliamentary system. The Pashtuns favoured the Presidential form while the other (Farsiwan) ethnic groups wanted a Federal Parliamentary system. The Americans pressure led to a highly centralised Presidential model. This may not be sustainable over time as it is far too dependent on one/two personalities with a pan-Afghan acceptance. To make the state more durable and inclusive it may have to evolve to a more Federal and Parliamentary form. The current state is highly centralised in theory but the ground reality is very different. The gap between theory and practice will have to be bridged.

ECONOMIC STRATEGIES

- So far Afghanistan has received some US$82 billion worth of assistance from the global community. The USA itself has provided US$32 billion worth of military and economic aid. India's contribution has been a little over a billion dollars worth of aid. China has pumped in US$3.2 billion for the Aynak Copper Mines Project.
- Afghanistan will need US$8 billion of aid a year for the next two decades - US$4 billion for the ANA and Police and US$4 billion of economic aid. The Afghan Govt's revenue in 2007 was just US$ 890 million a year whereas the expenditure on the ANA and Police itself was over US$ 2 billion per year.
- India should therefore encourage the USA/NATO and other countries to stay engaged in Afghanistan. This nation state that acted as a buffer between empires was deliberately destroyed in the Cold War competition. This state will have to be stabilized. Ungoverned spaces in the heart of Asia will become Somalia like bases for non-state actors that could destabilize peace and security at the global level.
- Should the US/NATO thin out deployment and reduce financial commitments India should take the lead in generating a regional consensus with Russia, Iran and Central Asia to stabilize the Afghan State.
- The Afghan economy must develop structural linkages with the Indian, Iranian and Central Asian Economies to become self sustaining.
- The Quantum and type of aid given by India so far is listed in Appendix A to this chapter. So far India is the fifth largest donor after US, UK, Japan and Germany. It has already executed projects worth US$750 million. These include the 218 km Delram-Jararanj highway that links Iran. It was gifted some 990 vehicles and provided one million tons of wheat in the form of high protein biscuits and India expanded the National TV network. It has completed the Salama Dam Power Project and is constructing the Afghan Parliament and the huge Indira Gandhi Hospital in Kabul.

- India should focus reconstruction efforts by private firms in the relatively stable Northern Provinces. Indian private sector could help in developing Iron, Copper and Gold Mines.
- India must focus on building infrastructure for expanding school level education as well as University Education Programmes. The emphasis must be on skilling the population for productive employment and doing capacity building.
- India must encourage the development of Small Scale Industries in Afghanistan.
- India must assist in the revival of Afghan agriculture and high value products like dry fruits, raisins and pomegranates.
- The farmers must be weaned off the farming of Poppy/opium by switching to high value crops like Dry fruits (Mc Dermott fruit as in the Golden Triangle) or Pomegranates.
- Indian Private Sector Companies must be encouraged to invest in Afghanistan. They could begin by investing in the relatively more stable provinces of Northern Afghanistan which are not as badly affected by the insurgency as the Pashtun areas. This could counter feelings of perceived neglect (by India) in these areas especially where ethnic minorities are concentrated.
- Afghanistan's agriculture had been totally dislocated by the large scale migration of the population and extensive mining of the area. With the return of the population Agriculture must revive and the temptation for less labour intensive crops like opium will be reduced.

MILITARY/QUASI MILITARY OPTIONS

- India's prime thrust area should be the capacity building of the ANA and Police. A 134,000 strong ANA is highly inadequate.
- India should offer to equip, train and pay for the following:
  - Up to two additional Afghan Infantry Divisions
  - A Brigade of Armour (based on old T-55 tanks)
  - A Brigade of Artillery (vintage 75/24 Howitzers/ 105 mm IFGs).

- Training Teams

  Army Training Team: This could be set up on the IMTRAT model either within Afghanistan or be located in Tajikistan/Uzbekistan. It should be adequately manned to be able to defend itself from any insurgent attacks and provide aid to the Afghan Govt in any emergency when so asked.

  Air Force Training Team/ Helicopter Training Unit: This could be co located, either in Afghanistan or a neighbouring country and train Afghan pilots for Jet aircraft and Helicopter flying. India could gift Jet Trainers and Dhruv/ M-17 helicopters.
- *Demining Assistance:* India could train Afghan Sappers and provide demining assistance through Indian Sapper teams under the aegis of the UN demining program.
- Construction of Secure Military Camps and infrastructure by the Indian Sappers as also construction of Advanced Landing Grounds/Helipads.
- Provision of Field Ambulance Companies for Medical Assistance.
- Establishment of supply nodes for Logistics Delivery.

INVOLVEMENT OF INDIAN TROOPS

The following guidelines should be kept in mind

- India will not be permitted to deploy troops while NATO/ISAF are in position in Afghanistan (in deference to Pakistani's sensitivities). This suits India as it prevents any feelings of hostility that may develop as a result of military operations/collateral damage while operating with the Americans.
- However should there be a major draw down of US/NATO troops (or even the remote possibility of a precipitate withdrawal), and there are indications of military intervention in Mufti by Pakistani troops, the situation would change materially.
- India should never commit ground troops inside Afghanistan in a stand alone mode. These must be part of a Regional Coalition or under the UN Flag. A unilateral Commitment of Indian Forces could give rise to a "Hari Singh Nalwa Syndrome" and would be exploited by the Pakistanis for propaganda purposes.

- Indian ability to assist the Afghan Govt militarily (in a post US withdrawal Scenario) is currently seriously constrained by lack of logistic routes/ capabilities.
- *Capacity Building through Iran* Should India wish to generate this option in a post US withdrawal scenario, India will have to work in close cooperation with Iran and develop access routes via the Iranian ports of Bandar Abbass and Chah Bahar. The Chah Bahar route though much shorter passes through Iranian Baluch areas which are affected by the Jundollah insurgency. The only viable route therefore is via Bandar Abbas. This will need to be developed in a major way before we even have the option to respond to any appeals for military support by the Afghan Govt (as part of the SAARC/Regional Arrangement or under the UN Charter.)
- *Air Support through Iran/Central Asia?* Should the Afghan Govt request for Air support, India would need Air Bases in Iran and Central Asian States like Tajikistan, Uzbekistan and Kyrgyzstan. These would necessitate developing a regional approach or using the assets of the Air Force Training Teams if established.
- *Op Jupiter Redux:* India must do feasibility study of providing support to extricate key Afghan Govt officials in a major emergency if the request is made in an extremity in a post US withdrawal scenario. The possibilities for the last three options are remote but cannot be wholly ignored.

Index